Contents

Bleeding
HEARTS

WRITTEN BY SCOTT HAY

 **FriesenPress**

Suite 300 - 990 Fort St
Victoria, BC, Canada, V8V 3K2
www.friesenpress.com

ISBN
978-1-4602-6052-4 (Hardcover)
978-1-4602-6053-1 (Paperback)
978-1-4602-6054-8 (eBook)

1. Biography & Autobiography, Personal Memoirs

Distributed to the trade by The Ingram Book Company

This book was written in loving memory of my father and is dedicated to my parents. I am the best of both of you. Thank you.

Chapter 1

December 3, 1997

7:00 a.m. The fuzzy radio blared and I scrambled blindly, trying to find the snooze button. My fingers floated over all the wrong buttons until I felt the one that would grant me temporary peace.

Disoriented and squinting, I grabbed a pair of jeans and a T-shirt from the floor—typical farmer attire. I got dressed, sat on the edge of my bed, and for a moment I pondered my day. It was going to be a busy one.

I had trouble opening my eyes as I stumbled out of my basement room to the stairs. Carefully finding each step, I walked upstairs and to the garage, where I threw on a smelly, dirty old coat and my insulated rubber boots, which fit like a glove. The crisp morning air hit me as I walked outside. It entered my lungs and gave me life. The winter morning was clear and brisk without snow. Blue skies stretched as far as I could see, with the exception of one cloud. It sat in the sky looking lost, almost as if it were asking me for direction. I looked at it and asked it for the same.

Out in our shop, I hopped in my dad's welding truck. It smelled like dust and cigarettes. Years of pipelining will do that to a vehicle. I backed the truck and the cattle trailer up to a holding pen to load a cow. She was a good old Hereford who had been on this farm as long as me, but she had been limping the last few days and it was getting worse. My dad and I suspected something was wrong with her foot, so we'd decided I would take her to the vet in Ponoka. I walked her into the trailer and slammed the back door shut. Jail doors closing.

As I headed back to the house for breakfast, I was greeted by the smell of cooked bacon. MMM... How I love bacon. I've been known to eat an entire pound in one sitting.

My mother was cooking while my father read the newspaper. "The Icemen won again last night," he said as he put the *Wetaskiwin Times* down.

"What was the score?" I asked.

"Six to two. That Jakobi kid got a hat trick. So I talked to Challand this morning. They're gonna need us for work next week."

"Well that's good news." I was fresh out of school and had just quit a job with my father's friend so my father and I could work together.

"Make sure you get that truck to the dealership in Ponoka for ten o'clock. We need that transmission fixed. Your mom and I are driving to town to see your grandparents. We should be back for dinner."

I finished eating and ran downstairs to change my clothes. A freshly ironed pair of boot cut Wranglers and a newer T-shirt were my garb for the day. When I came back upstairs, my father was waiting for me. "You all set to go?"

"Yep."

"When you get back from Ponoka, you can have the afternoon for yourself to do whatever you want," he said with a big grin on his face. There was pride and appreciation in his voice.

I felt that this was his way of saying I was now a man. I had just turned eighteen, and my father had been treating me with a new respect. Putting on my cowboy boots, I held my head high. With a sense of pride and confidence I looked him in the eye and nodded.

"Goodbye, Dad."

The sun shone on my face as I drove into Ponoka. I smiled, feeling complete independence for the first time. My parents had always given me and my brother and sister independence, but this was different. Now, no one was looking over my shoulder to ask me what I was doing or to tell me to do things differently. For the first time in my life, I felt as if I were the boss.

After pulling into town, I found the vet clinic, located behind the KFC just off the main drag. A white building with green lettering read, Ponoka Veterinary Clinic. Dr. Thompson greeted me as I walked in, and I explained that I had to take the truck to the shop for ten a.m.

"Could I leave the cattle trailer and the cow here until the truck's finished getting repaired?"

"Not a problem, Scott," he said with a smile, "but you have to help me get this cow out of the trailer and into the clinic so I can take a look at her."

Grinning back, I told him I would gladly help. I backed the trailer up to the clinic's Dutch doors, and as Dr. Thompson and I walked the cow into the building, we talked like a pair of old farmers. We discussed the weather, how moderate the fall had been, the slow start to the winter, when the snow would come, and of course, my favourite hockey team, the Edmonton Oilers. As we dug the dirt from the bottom of the cow's hoof, Dr.

Thompson spotted something sticking out of the bottom. "What is it?" I asked.

He grabbed a pair of jumbo-sized tweezers, carefully pulled out the object, and examined it. "A small sliver of steel. This old girl must have stepped on it sometime in the last week." Since the object was old and rusted, I was unable to tell exactly what it was. More than likely it had been lying on the ground since my grandfather owned the farm.

"You must feel relieved, you old girl," I said, patting the cow's back.

By this time it was almost ten, so I said goodbye to Dr. Thompson, unhooked the cattle trailer, and headed to the Dodge dealership which was near by. When I walked in, it was quiet— almost haunting. I walked through the building to the service department, where they told me that the truck would take two to four hours to fix.

Now what? I wondered, knowing I would get bored and restless. While deciding how to kill a few hours, I looked at the new trucks. One in particular grabbed my attention—a bright-yellow, short box 4x4 Sport. *Wow, what a hot truck!* I thought, looking it up and down, dreaming of cruising in it and turning heads. *I would have no problem finding a hottie to ride with me.* While I stared at this work of art, a man from the service department approached me.

"We don't have the right parts for the truck in stock. We're unable to fix that transmission today. We ordered the parts and they'll be in next week."

My first thought was, *My dad is going to chew these guys a new asshole for wasting time*, and then I realized I had the whole day to myself. *Wow!* Suddenly I was excited. I felt like jumping up and yelling, "Yes!"

I hopped in the truck, sped back to the veterinary clinic, and ran inside. Then, Dr. Thompson and I walked the old cow into the trailer. Dr. Thompson hardly had time to hand me a bill before I was on my way.

During the twenty-minute ride home, I cranked the stereo and listened to Steve Earl. He was one of my dad's favourites. As I sang along to "Guitar Town," I felt free, as if I were on a vacation. I had never been on a vacation, but I guessed this was what it would feel like. I thought about going riding on the quad, fishing, or even into the city to catch a movie. Whom would I call when I got home? What was I going to do? My mind was racing. I was wound up, ready to do something besides work.

Still singing, I pulled off Highway 611—just four miles of gravel road to go. The sound of rocks pinging off the cattle trailer was my music until I pulled into the driveway. But my heart sank when I saw my parents' car sitting in front of the garage. "Fuck!" I shouted, knowing that if my dad knew I was home this early, he would give me some sort of work to do. The problem with living on a farm is that something always has to be done; there's always a fence to be fixed, or a tree to trim, or a piece of machinery to maintain. *This fucking sucks.* I took a deep breath, swung the truck around, and backed it up to one of our holding pens to unload the cow. My mom was standing outside on our lawn beside the car, which I noticed was running. "If I had only driven home slower or messed around in town a little, I would've missed them," I muttered.

I slid off the seat and out of the truck. That's when I saw that the tractor was parked behind the Quonset, with the loader all the way up. This struck me as odd for two reasons: one, the entire time we owned the farm, the tractor had never been parked behind the Quonset, and two, it is an unspoken rule among farmers that you never leave the loader all the way up in the air. I looked over to my mom and saw an odd look of fear on her face. She was crying slightly. I had been raised in a very tough home—not many tears were shed in our family, so this worried me. I ran up to her, afraid of what I was going to hear.

In a trembling voice, she told me my father was missing.

"Well where did he go?" I quickly asked.

Regaining her composure, she replied, "He went for a walk this morning and never came back."

I breathed out slowly in relief. "Oh, that's no problem. I'll go find him." A load lifted off my chest. My father would often go for long walks and would sometimes stop at the neighbours' for coffee. He would be gone for hours some days. I reassured my mother that everything was going to be okay and that I would go find him.

After unloading our old cow, my mother approached me and said. "Take the quad to the neighbours' and see if he's over there having coffee,"

"Will do."

Hustling into our Quonset, I got on the quad, and hit the road. I planned to stop at a pig farmer's house first. He and his wife were a cute, old couple who lived on an equally old farm, and my grandparents and parents had been friends with them for a long time. They lived a couple of miles from our place, so it took me several minutes to get there. When I pulled into their driveway, old John Bently was just sauntering to the house. I drove up beside him and asked him if he had seen my dad.

"No I haven't," he replied. "Is everything alright?"

"No problems. Dad went for a walk and we're just trying to track him down. My mom's waiting for him so they can go to town to see my grandparents."

"Oh, I'm sure he's around here somewhere." He knew how my father would wander around the countryside so he wasn't worried about the situation.

I left John's and drove to see Doyle and Carol Podiski, a couple my parents hung out with once in a while. I pulled up to their old trailer, and Carol was outside smoking on the deck.

She seemed quite surprised to see me.

"Oh hey, Scott, what are you doing here?"

I told her the story and she looked concerned, but I reassured her that everything was okay. She told me that if she saw or heard from him, she would let us know.

Driving home, I kept a keen eye on the fields, expecting to see my dad wandering around analyzing them. This is what we called "farmer driving": the art of driving down a road without looking at it because you are looking in the fields. I was already an expert—I had been doing it for as long as I had been driving. The closer I got to home, the more slowly I drove. I found myself growing a bit concerned. As I approached our house, my mother was coming in from the field, in the tractor. Thinking my father was with her, I raced to greet her.

She stopped the tractor and I climbed up into the cab.

"Have you seen him?" I asked.

"Well no. He wasn't at the neighbours'?"

"No. I checked both the Bentlys' and the Podiskis' houses. What are you doing out here with the tractor?"

"I was just putting some straw bales in the dead animal pit. The horses were running in the area and I didn't want them to fall in and break their legs."

We had just put the horses out in that field the day before. When the hole was full or stunk too much, we would fill it in with earth. Until then, it remained an open pit.

I headed back to the farmyard and parked the quad. Then I just stood there, puzzled, trying to solve the riddle. *Where is my dad?* I slowly walked to the truck, drove it to the shop, then carefully backed the trailer in and unhooked it, my mind focused on the riddle. My mother brought the tractor into the shop too, parked it, and climbed down.

"What now?" I asked.

"Take the quad and go look in our fields."

Without hesitation I got back on the quad and drove off. I sped to the north field entrance and from there, worked my way south. I made wide swaths up and down the hay field. All the crops were gone because the fall harvest was over and winter was beginning, so I knew it would be easy to see him. The fields were just stubble. My mind raced—I was scared of what I might find. All I could think was that I was going to find him dead from a heart attack. But that didn't make sense because my father was only thirty-nine years old and in good health. I slowly cruised from one field to the next, but found nothing. With a sense of panic and a sinking feeling in my stomach, I drove back to our house along the gravel road, searching the ditches. At home, I parked right in front of the house and ran inside, where my mother was doing dishes. She was washing the knives and cutting boards we had used a couple of days before to butcher a wild boar I had shot.

My stomach was a little uneasy, but I knew I had to eat, so I grabbed some leftovers from the fridge. The house was silent. Deep in thought, I ate my lunch and continued trying to solve the worrisome puzzle in my head. Where was my father? Where could he have gone? Why were there no vehicles missing? What had happened to him?

After lunch I went to use the bathroom. As I sat down on the toilet, I stared at the floor and noticed a small, rectangular hole in the linoleum between my feet. It was the width of a Bic pen and the length of a stamp. *That's weird*, I thought. Having sat on this toilet many times before, I knew the hole was new. When I stood, I noticed the plastic windowsill was broken on the window directly to my left. My mind began working in high gear. Why was the sill broken? Why was there a hole in the linoleum?

When I went and asked my mom these questions, she replied, "The other day I was washing the window and had trouble getting it out. The sill broke when I was yanking on the glass trying to remove it. When it popped out, it fell out of my hand and the corner of the window landed on the floor. Even though it left a small hole in the floor, I was just happy the windowpane didn't break."

"That was lucky," I replied with a chuckle. "So what were you doing today when Dad went missing?"

"I was taking a bath and getting ready to go to town. Then I pulled the car out of the garage, thinking your dad would be outside, ready to go. And that's when you came home."

At this point I realized she knew about as much as I did. Which was nothing.

She continued. "What doesn't make sense is that his wallet is still on the nightstand."

My mind started working like a hamster on a wheel; running round and round and ending up nowhere. If Dad had gone out with a friend, or for some weird reason was running away, he would have taken his wallet.

I stood there motionless, staring off into space, not knowing which way to turn or which way to go.

"Hmm," I finally said. "Well I'm gonna go outside and keep looking."

Just then, the phone rang. My mother suspected it would be my grandmother and quickly told me not to mention my father's disappearance. We agreed it would be best not to worry her until we knew for sure that something was wrong.

I answered, and my grandmother asked me if I was coming into town with my parents.

"No, we had a problem with a cow, so Mom and Dad are cancelling their trip to town today. They'll call you later tonight to reschedule."

With no suspicion in her voice, my grandmother made a little small talk and then let me go. ·

Relieved that she hadn't asked too many questions, I tried to figure out my next move. I wandered to our front yard and then around to the north side of the house, where there were several trees. My eyes scanned the landscape for clues. Then I spotted something different about the house. By the bathroom window, on the north side of the house, the stucco on the wall was smashed in—nothing big; just a hole the size of a baseball. When I took a closer look, I noticed tractor tire marks near the house. This didn't make any sense, because I knew it would have taken a lot of effort to get the tractor into that area. It was also a tight squeeze, so whoever had been driving had to have been a veteran tractor driver. Brushing it off as unimportant, I walked down a path in the trees leading to our horse-riding pen. My eyes were sharp. I looked into the old outhouse along the path and with a little hesitation, peeked down the hole of the toilet. I almost expected something to jump out, as though I were in a horror movie, but nothing happened. After walking across the horse-riding arena, I jumped the fence and headed briskly to a cattle shed, and then to our barn before proceeding to check every crack of every shed we owned. I searched every piece of equipment, and even the hayloft in the barn. I searched the granaries and every old car parked in our yard.

Panic set in; that sinking feeling in the gut that indicates something is very wrong. I wondered if my father had any enemies, or if anything had been different about his behaviour, but I kept drawing blanks. He was a likeable man, and he was in shape. I jogged back to the house to pick up the quad. Knowing I was going to be driving for a while during my next search, I pulled up to our bulk fuel tank and popped the seat off the quad. Still boggled, I slowly filled the tank. Gas spilling over onto the ground snapped me out of my trance. The fumes entered my lungs, and like a machine, I felt fuelled up—ready to operate.

I drove up and down each and every ditch within a one-mile radius of our home. If he was in the ditch, there was a one hundred percent chance I would see him. Though I wanted to find him, part of me didn't want to be the one to find him if he was dead. I didn't want that image stuck in my mind. A tear rolled down my face at the thought. But, doing what I had always been taught, I fought back the tears and buried all my emotions. I was a soldier at war searching for a lost comrade. I had to be strong.

I squeezed the handlebars so tightly I felt my calluses roll between the grips and my hands. It was now around four p.m. I had a feeling that if he wasn't found within the next hour, he would be found dead.

I returned to our fields again, knowing this was where most of his walks took place. This time, I drove in tighter swaths, taking approximately twenty-foot runs up and down each field. I knew I couldn't miss him this time. The stubble from our harvested crops popped and broke beneath the tires. My senses were heightened and sharp. My eyes scanned the earth in the failing light. Moving from our hayfield, to our grain field, and into our other hayfield, I found nothing.

I searched our hay pen, where there were hundreds of bales from our successful harvest. Quickly walking up and down the rows stacked two high, I searched every crack and crevasse. Then I hurried over to the pen with the horses and the dead animal pit. Walking through the brush I saw nothing but the thousands of rocks we had picked from our fields and thrown into the pen. The rocks reminded me of an ancient Aboriginal burial ground.

As I wandered around the dead animal pit, I noticed a washtub we used to hold scrap meat had been placed between the wall of the pit and the straw bales. I wanted to grab it and take it back to the house, where it belonged, but since I was in a hurry, I decided to come back and get it another day. Getting back on the quad, I hauled ass back to the house. The failed hunt had left me feeling skunked.

My twelve-year-old sister, Michelle, got off the school bus just as I returned to the yard. As soon as I told her what was happening, she instantly started looking for our missing father. Walking nervously through the trees across the road from the house, she called out for him.

Back in the house, my mom was in the process of doing what she always did: cleaning, washing clothes, and cooking.

"I'm pretty worried about Dad," I told her as I walked in. "I think something's wrong. We should call the police soon."

"Let's eat dinner first," she said.

I figured we were just buying a little more time, hoping he would show up or call.

"Why is the old white washtub in the dead animal pit?" I asked.

"I took it out there to empty your wild boar scraps when I put those bales in the pit. I must have forgot it because I was worried about your dad."

"Oh. So what's up with the tractor tracks on the north side of the house? And there's a hole in the house's stucco. It's weird—it looks like it's the shape and size of a tractor bucket tooth." I felt like a detective; working with my mother, trying to find clues and hints that would lead us in the right direction.

"Your dad and I were planning to buy a satellite dish that mounts on the roof. We used the tractor to plan where we were going to put it. When your dad pulled up to the house, he hit it with one of the tractor bucket teeth."

On the farm, we had only three channels to choose from. My father had been talking about getting us a satellite for a long time, so I was happy to hear he was taking steps toward purchasing it. I should have been jumping up and down with joy, but my mind was too preoccupied. I told my mom I was going back outside for one last look before it got completely dark.

Outside, my sister's voice came from the north, calling for my dad. I mounted the quad and drove up the road in that direction, finding her across the road in the trees on our neighbours' property. Her voice was scared but firm. To make sure I didn't lose her too, and to show her she wasn't alone in the search, I joined her. I could see in her eyes that she knew something was wrong. My heart felt for her. It had been beating like a hummingbird's wings all day, but the sadness in her eyes slowed it down and grounded me.

It was time to stop looking.

Darkness had set in along with my feeling of defeat. I stood paralyzed. A bomb could have been dropped and I wouldn't have flinched. I felt as though I had failed my father and an immense sadness took over. My mouth watered, and my jaw trembled slightly. I clenched it and slowly closed my eyes to fight back tears as I took a deep breath. The search was over, but I had to be strong and not show fear in front of my sister.

"Michelle, it's time to go in," I called out.

She answered with a very slow, long, "Okay." We doubled up on the quad back to the house, went inside, and washed up for dinner. Mom served us at the dining room table, then continued cleaning. I saw that she was keeping busy to hide the pain; to be strong for us children. The house was as silent as a graveyard. Eerie. We sat there, empty and worried, while trying to eat. I knew some sort of action had to be taken. In the eighteen years of my existence, nothing like this had ever happened to my family. We were very predictable and reliable people.

I was now the man of the house. I had to take charge and show leadership.

"Mom, it's time to call the police. We have to file a missing person report."

"That's a good idea. Call your grandparents and your aunts and uncles too."

I picked up the phone and dialled the police. I told them that my dad had gone for a walk in the morning and never returned, that all the vehicles were accounted for, and that his wallet was still sitting on his nightstand. I felt I had done my job leading up to this moment. I had left no stone unturned on that farm.

"Did you spend any time looking for your father?" they asked.

"Of course," I said firmly, following with a light chuckle shaking my head. I could have screamed at the lady for asking such a stupid question, but I needed her cooperation. I told her I had searched all of our fields and every shed and granary on our property, and I certainly didn't leave out the fact that I had spent hours driving up and down the fields, and walking through the surrounding trees. I gave her our farm's legal land location and general directions to it from Wetaskiwin. She told me she would send a couple of cruisers out to ask us more questions and see what kind of help they could be in finding my father.

Then it was time to call my grandparents. This call would be tough because they would have so many questions to which I didn't have answers. Pacing back and forth with the cordless phone in hand, I dialled their number. My grandma answered, and I told her she should come out to the farm. When she asked me why, I hesitantly told her the news. I tried to keep the conversation short to avoid the barrage of questions. I told her we were going to gather friends and family to determine a search plan.

Sounding distraught, she said, "We're on our way."

Then I called my aunt, and after her, a couple of our neighbours. I asked them all the same questions: "Have you seen my father today?—Have you heard from him in the last twelve hours?" Friends and family knew my father; they knew something was wrong. One by one, people arrived at our house, willing to do anything to help and to give my family moral support. Before the police even arrived, our house was full of people drinking pots of coffee and trying to solve the mystery of the missing man. They picked apart clues and asked my mother and me the same questions over and over. But none of it mattered because nothing was bringing us closer to a solution.

The first police officers arrived and told me more were on the way. They had a lot of questions for me, and I told them everything I knew. Finally everyone just chatted and gossiped to keep their minds off the problem. One officer started talking to me about hunting African animals. He had known a man who had hunted "the big five." This had always been a dream of mine, and I should have had piles of questions for him, but I was blank. I was polite and smiled and nodded, but it all went in one ear and out the other. My father was missing. Nothing else mattered.

Chapter 2

The Storm Before the Storm

I was born in the fall of 1979. My parents wanted to name me Donald, but my grandmother pushed for Scott. Since I shared my birthday with my grandfather, and my father's respect for him was second to none, I was given my grandfather's name as my middle name. I'm proud to be called Scott Leonard Hay.

My older brother Mike had been born in October 1976. Though conceived before marriage, he was born after the wedding. We lived in an apartment in Edmonton for my first couple of years on this planet. Then my grandparents gifted an acreage to my father near the town of Wetaskiwin, four miles east of my grandparents' farm. My grandfather owned the land surrounding our acreage, so we had all the space in the world in which to keep active. Our parents always made us play outside. Our driveway was close to a quarter-mile long, and we would ride bikes up and down it all day to our heart's content. The mobile home we lived in was situated atop a large hill, which helped us out greatly with summer fun. We would connect two bright, banana-yellow Slip'N Slides to form one long one and spend sunny days sliding down the hill and running back up. Some of my greatest memories are of riding bikes up and down that driveway and sliding up and down that hill. I'm grateful for those experiences—every child deserves these kinds of memories.

Living on that acreage was fun, and I remember it as a place of freedom and peace. It was surrounded by trees and pasture land, and made a perfect backdrop for many adventures. Playing GI Joe in the trees was always exciting, and Dukes of Hazard in the smashed-up old Dodge Charger was equally as thrilling. There was also a slough for us to play in, and we were forever catching frogs and tadpoles to take back to the house as pets. I'm sure my mom loved this. We always came back with our skin and clothing soaked in mud. I hope to one day raise children in an atmosphere like this.

My childhood there was stimulating. The chores were minimal and my parents rarely fought. Life was easy, and I seldom got spankings. But I'll never forget my first. I was around the ripe age of three and repeating everything I heard. My parents had some friends over and the guests had brought their kids. While the adults were drinking and playing cards, I listened to them talking and repeated some of the curse words. This sparked quite a reaction among my peers, and like any child who receives attention I wanted more. So I continued, shouting out "Fuck!" and giggling. The other kids laughed, giving me more reason to continue. My parents scolded me, but I kept on performing. When our company left, my father stormed into the bedroom, where my mother was putting me to sleep. "Cursing is not for little boys!" he shouted, then he grabbed me by the hand and yanked my arm in the air so my feet barely touched the ground. He started swatting my ass yelling, "Don't you ever say those bad words again."

I felt as if I would go flying in the air every time he swatted my ass. It would have been a fun ride if it hadn't hurt so much. That day, a seed of fear was planted in me. I started thinking about the repercussions of misbehaving. The seed kept me on a straight line of good behaviour for the most part, because I knew what was coming if I wandered off it.

In July 1985, my parents got what every mom and dad of two boys wants: a little girl. Michelle was a cutie from birth, and Mom and Dad's little princess. My mother made her new dresses for every occasion, and my father gave her whatever she wanted. But she was trouble, mostly because of her innocence and curiosity.

When Michelle was three and I was nine, I came home from school one afternoon to find my new kitten dead. I was really upset because the mother cat had only had two, and one had already died. I needed to figure out what had happened. It had been in perfect health in the morning when I left. My gut told me my sister had something to do with it, so I instantly blamed her. At three years old she already knew just to deny, deny, deny.

Like a good cop or lawyer in a movie, I drilled her over and over, each time more intensely than before. I assumed this tactic would work on a three-year-old, and I waited for her to break down. She held strong though, and after all of my finger pointing, it was decided that the kitten's death was a mystery.

After a few hours passed, my little sister came out of her room with her head down, crying. Trying to get the words out past her sobbing, she muttered, "I was giving him a bear hug and bubbles came out of his nose." I knew it! Murderer! From that day on, my relationship with Michelle was always a love-hate one. I loved my little sister, but I hated the things she did.

We were raised in a close family atmosphere. I saw my grand-parents a few times a week and my aunts and uncles and cousins usually once a week. Every holiday or birthday we gathered for a big dinner and to play games. We went to Mount Red Park for afternoon picnics, or my grandparents parked their motorhome at the lake and we all visited. Sometimes we even packed nine or ten of us into my grandparents' Suburban to go to town for Chinese food. Whenever there were cows to be chased or vaccinated, the whole family got together and helped. Butchering them was also a family event. Since we had our own meat-cutting station on the farm, the entire family gathered to cut their year's worth of meat in one day. Everyone had a job. The oldest men shot and skinned the steer, and cut the meat into steaks and roasts with the band saw. The women cut the meat off the bones and separated the meat from the fat. With the help of the older women, a couple of children ground beef into hamburger, and helped the women wrap the meat into packages and mark them. It was quite an operation, and it ran smoothly—all family, and all fun. My family was a lot closer than we are now, but I'm lucky to have grown up with strong ties to family.

Everything changed when I was in grade six. My grandparents wanted to retire and move to town, so my father stepped up to the plate and purchased their farm to keep it in the family. Even at my young age, I knew it was a workload I didn't want.

The first year wasn't bad. We didn't have many cows or much machinery, so we rented the land out and the chores were manageable. But as time passed, we slowly acquired tractors, a haybine, hay rakes, grain augers, a grain truck, a disc, harrows, a combine, etc. More machinery meant more work. And as my father acquired more machinery, he also acquired more cows. We started out with twenty head of cattle, most of which were my grandfather's. Later we would have close to seventy in our herd. We started out with two hundred and forty acres of land, and at our peak we were at five hundred and sixty. The amount of work grew, and with the growth came stress. My brother and I had never worked on a farm before, and it seemed as if my father just expected us to know everything the day he purchased it. We made mistakes regularly, and then came the consequences. Usually my father lost his temper, and violence erupted.

Times got tougher when my brother graduated from high school and left for college. My father worked out of town most of the year, leaving my mother and me to take care of the farm. The workload was heavy for a sixteen-year-old. Most of my summer days were spent on the tractor. I would be up at seven a.m. and was lucky if I was back home from the field by nine p.m. If I wasn't in the field, there were always other jobs to do.

Some of the jobs were awful, like shovelling grain. When the temperature was thirty degrees Celsius, a hot, stuffy grain bin filled with dust was the last place I wanted to be. One day my father and I were shovelling grain in the bin, and it was hard to see anything with all the dust particles floating around. When my father was around it was always a head-down-ass-up working attitude. If he didn't think I was trying my hardest, he would give me a smack or a kick in the ass. On this particular day, the truck box lifted too high, and some of the grain spilled over the box and onto the ground. I quickly jumped out of the bin and lowered the box to stop it from spilling over even more. Ignoring everything that was going on, from the machinery that was running, to the grain that had just been spilled, my father lost his mind on me.

He rushed out of the bin screaming, telling me I should have been watching the box. Then he started slapping me in the head and proceeded to throw me to the ground, where he kicked me in the ribs with his steel-toe boots. I rolled away, trying to get some distance so I could stand up, but my father moved as I moved and repeatedly kicked me in the stomach and ribs to keep me down. I'm sure it would have hurt a lot more if my adrenalin hadn't been pumping. All I could think of was trying to stand up to end the beating. But the fact of the matter was, my ass-kicking wouldn't be over until my dad decided it was over. When he finally let me stand up, I felt the pain throughout my body. My back, ribs, stomach, and arms throbbed, but I could never cry. If I did, my father would say, "I'll give you something to cry about," and hit me again.

At times like this I hated my father. I knew it was equally his fault that day for not seeing the grain overflowing. Often he would be the one to mess up, but in a rage he would hit me anyway.

One Christmas before we went to my grandparents' for a family dinner and gift exchange, I mentioned to my father that the snowmobile wasn't running properly. He, Mike, and I went outside to see if we could fix the problem. Small parts, tight spaces, and big hands are not a good combination. It was only a matter of minutes until my father was yelling and blaming all the problems on me.

"What the fuck did you do to the Ski-Doo?"

"Nothing!"

"Well you obviously did something. The thing's fucked up!"

I was bent down looking at the motor when *whack!* Out of nowhere my father backhanded me in the face. My head whipped sideways into the hood of the Ski-Doo. I was grateful it was cold outside—my pain was quickly numbed by the weather.

"You fucking idiot. You can fix this when we get home from town. Go in the house and get ready for dinner at Grandma's."

When I walked inside, my mother looked at me with a tear in her eye and sympathetically asked, "What's wrong? What did you do now?"

"Nothing," I said in disbelief.

"Go get cleaned up. There's blood running down your face." As she walked away, she muttered under her breath, "Jesus Christ, it's Christmas!"

Downstairs in the bathroom, I looked in the mirror. My cheek had a three-inch slice down the side. *Merry Fucking Christmas*, I thought as I washed the blood away. I felt as if a dark cloud was hovering over me and I couldn't get out from under it. At my grandparents' I lied to my family about why my face was scratched. No one questioned me or my parents about it. I don't know if anyone had any idea of the abuse occurring in our household. But even if they had, I'm confident nothing would have been done to stop it. We Hays generally never talked about our problems or got involved in each other's business.

The violence was usually a result of something so small that by the next day, I couldn't remember why I had been hit or yelled at. It was at its worst when my father was trying to quit smoking. He was always on edge, ready to freak out. I guess the stress of not having a cigarette was more than I could ever imagine. At this point in my life I was fifteen, scared of my father and did everything I could to avoid him. He seemed out of control, and I spent a few months on edge, tiptoeing around him, trying not to set him off into a blind rage. Though I was scared of being beat up, I knew his dedicated love would stop him from killing me.

During this time, I was almost failing two classes. When report card day came, I was worried about what my father would do. I had hope that my body would remain intact. My grandmother had been staying with us for a couple of days, and I knew that if I showed my father the report card when she was there, he wouldn't attack. I stepped off the school bus, and as I walked down the driveway, I could see her red and black Suburban parked in front of our house. A sigh of relief calmed my body. She was at the door to greet me, but unfortunately, she had just been waiting for her grandchildren to come home so she could say goodbye before she left.

This is so bad, I thought.

After she was gone, I quickly escaped to my room to change my clothes before doing chores. I knew my parents knew it was report card day, and as I came upstairs, I felt as if I were on death row—a dead man walking. My father asked me for my report card, and I got that sinking feeling in my stomach. Stalling, I slowly walked back downstairs to my room to get it. As I walked upstairs for the second time, a greater fear set in.

After looking it over, he started with some minor yelling and name-calling. "I don't know how you can be so dumb. I swear to God if your brains were dynamite, you couldn't even blow your fucking nose." Then his voice got louder and louder as his blood hit the boiling point. "If shit meant no brains, you would be a fucking pile of it!" He continued screaming as he walked towards me. "I swear to God, I don't know how my son can be such a moron. You're a fucking idiot!"

That's when it happened. He wound up and open-palmed the side of my head. Then he grabbed me by my neck and my feet left the ground. In one fell swoop, he choke-slammed me to the kitchen floor while continuing to scream at me about how stupid I was. Winded, I tried to pick my body up off the floor. As I scrambled to my hands and knees, he hit me with a swift, hard soccer kick to the stomach. It hurt much more than anything he had ever done. My stomach muscles contracted and I curled up in a ball of pain. Continuing, he grabbed me by the back of my shirt and tried to make me stand up straight. I couldn't...It felt as though my stomach were being ripped in two. The pain was unbearable. I stood hunched over, on the verge of falling.

My mother tried to step in.

"Bruce, stop! This has to stop," she pleaded.

He slapped her across the face and screamed, "Shut the fuck up, bitch, and mind your own business or you'll be next!" Then he grabbed my mother, my brother, and me and kicked us all out of the house as he yelled about how useless we were. Because Michelle was "Daddy's little girl," she stayed in the house with him.

My mother cried as we walked to the Quonset. "Why can't you guys just do better?"

After twenty minutes, we decided enough time had passed and Dad had probably cooled down enough for us to try to mend things. We walked in and saw him playing darts with my little sister at the bottom of the stairs. "Bruce, we can't do this," my mother pleaded.

My father just looked at me and said, "You'd better straighten up or you'll be out of here."

Poof! Just like magic, the fight was over, and we all acted as if nothing happened. Like most of our fights, it was never spoken of again.

I've been hit in the head, stomach, and chest. I've had my body slammed through the kitchen table and my legs taken out from under me with a cattle cane. I've been whipped with a willow branch, thrown out of a tractor, and much more. But no matter what my father did to me, I always forgave him, and I will always continue to forgive him. Why? Because I know it wasn't me he was truly mad at. I know he was fighting his own inner demons. I know deep inside, his love for me was stronger than he was.

Though I always forgave him, his continued abuse pissed me off. I felt that he never recognized or appreciated all of the work I did on the farm, especially after my brother moved away and my mother and I ran the show. I would have school from eight-thirty in the morning until three-thirty in the afternoon, and some days I worked after school at a local carpenter's shop. If I didn't, I would have to come home and feed the cows or work the fields. In the winter, I had to check on our cows every two hours for any sign of a calf soon to be born. There were some real nasty nights when the cows had problems calving. I would be up all night, then go to school all day and work all the next night.

I hated those cows. I clearly remember one day in spring when we were vaccinating them before putting them out to pasture. One cow kept swishing her shit-covered tail in my father's face every time he got close to giving her the needle. "Grab her tail," he yelled at me. I had been following the golden rule of farming: Never stand behind an animal. They kick. A few seconds passed, and I still hadn't gotten hold of her tail. My father yelled at me again, but the cow kept swishing it away. Suddenly my father grabbed me, threw me right into the back end of the cow, and yelled, "Grab her fucking tail!" The cow's instant response was a kick to my gut. I flew back a couple of yards and hit the ground in pain. My father snapped and grabbed a heavy steel pipe, with which he beat the cow's leg until he calmed down. He left her with a limp. For the next week, every night after school I had to chase the cow into the chute to give her medicine to help her leg heal. That was extra work I never needed. Ninety percent of the time when we were vaccinating cows, I ended up getting my ass kicked, or at least got screamed at.

Those times were tiring and tough. I was run down from all work and no sleep. Any chance I had I would rest my eyes—on the bus, in class, at home, and even while driving. An angel must have been watching over me one night while I was driving home. I was only three miles from home when I fell asleep at the wheel. A loud thud woke me up. I never saw what I hit. I looked at my speedometer. It only went to 160 kilometres per hour, and the needle was buried past that mark. My foot never left the pedal until I got home. When I got out of the truck, I found the front end smashed up, full of deer hair and bone debris. I was too tired to worry about it that night and went to bed.

After coming in from doing chores the next morning, I told my father about hitting the deer. He wasn't mad, but he never knew the severity of the incident. At the speed I was going, if I had hit the ditch, my truck would have flipped over at least two or three times, and there's a good chance I would have been killed that night.

It still amazes me that I was able to function at that time. I often think that I could never work that hard now, for so many hours. I don't think my father ever recognized how much I did, or how hard I was working. I know he was proud of the man I was becoming, but he never gave me the respect I knew I deserved for giving my soul to that farm. I wish he had shown his appreciation more, so I had felt less like a slave.

For every one of my father's bad qualities though, he had good ones. He was still a loving and caring father who provided for his children. He taught me how to be a man and what makes a man. When I was a kid, he taught me how to make a fire and chop wood. As I grew older, it was how to shoot a gun and hit a running target. He taught me how to skin a deer and get it ready for butchering.

He taught me how to ride my first bike, and after that, he showed me how to ride a dirt bike and an ATV, and how to drive a vehicle in snow and mud. Not long after that I was driving tractors and grain trucks. He took his time teaching me how to drive these different vehicles and showing me how to maintain them. When I was four I was checking the air in my bike tires and oiling the chain. By the time I was eight I was fuelling the ATV and greasing the joints on our vehicles. When I was fourteen I could do full oil and lube and tire rotations on a vehicle, and small maintenance issues were never a problem. Around this time, my father also taught me how to weld. My welding teacher in school didn't know much and didn't take the time to show the class what he knew, but when I came home my father would fire up his welding rig and teach me the basics. He was a very hands-on teacher. He was always building stuff for our farm, and my brother and I were always right by his side. We were his helpers, and he taught us responsibility and pride in workmanship. I was proud to have Bruce Hay as my father.

I was close with both my parents, but in different ways. My father and I bonded over "manly" things like hunting and fishing, while my mother and I would play games and talk. But I wasn't comfortable telling either of them my secrets or thoughts—I always feared getting in trouble. I wanted to talk to them about how much I hated the farm, and the pressure I was under to do well in school. I wanted to talk to them about my workload and lack of sleep. I wanted to talk to them about moving out, and maybe staying at a friend's house. I knew that if I did that, it would keep my relationship with both parents strong, and this way, I wouldn't have to endure any abuse. I wanted to talk to them about the depression I felt from always being verbally and mentally abused, and about how at times I felt life would be better if I were dead. I wanted to talk to them about how I thought the greatest revenge I could bestow on my father for his abuse would be killing myself and leaving him a note telling him it was his fault. Instead, I said nothing.

I had the right to remain silent. I was in solitary confinement, a dark hole without a light.

I sometimes thought about running away. But where would I go? I needed financial stability, and I needed it fast. As a teenager, my wages were not good enough to allow me to make it in the real world. I needed more, so I got involved with a friend who was distributing stolen stereo equipment. My bedroom was filled with thousands of dollars worth of equipment, but my parents were naive as to what was going on. One night my father asked me about a speaker I was taking into my room, and I told him it was a friend's and I was just trying it out. He believed me and had no reason to question me.

It was most obvious at school that something shady was happening. Only about twenty kids drove to school each day, and of those twenty, only ten had their own vehicles. Of those ten, eight had competition-grade sound systems worth over five thousand dollars. Luckily, in the countryside, nobody ever suspects anything illegal is going on, so we never got in trouble.

I was finishing high school, and my freedom was near. I knew that when I left, my mother's workload would become unmanageable. I didn't care. Call it selfish or call it survival—I wanted out. I didn't really have my future planned. I had always thought that a position as a radio or television broadcaster would suit me because I loved music, liked to talk, enjoyed entertaining, and felt that the fame that came with the job would help me leave my mark on this earth. But my school counsellor told me to forget about the idea. I had all of the minimum requirements to get into school, but he told me I shouldn't pursue it. He thought I would struggle. Thinking back on it now, I never should have listened to him. I am a good public speaker, I carry an entertaining energy with me, and I would have been great on air.

Like everyone else in Alberta, my back-up plan was the oil patch. I just wanted to get away from the farm and my father. In the late summer of 1997, one of my dad's best friends called our house looking for a welder's helper. The timing could not have been better and I was off to Bonnyville, Alberta, to help build a gas plant. Don was a nice, easygoing guy, and his calm demeanour was the change I needed. Working with him helped me clear my mind, and I hoped that my absence would make my father appreciate all the hard work I had done around the farm.

I worked for Don for over three months and spent my eighteenth birthday in Bonnyville. It was a fun crew, but Bonnyville was boring. Don's wife was expecting a child near the end of October, and it was decided that as soon as she went into labour, we would pack the truck and go home for a week. On October 30th at 10:15 a.m., Don went to check his phone. When his head popped out of the truck, he was smiling the biggest grin I had ever seen on this man. Chewing tobacco dripped from his lip as he yelled, "Scotty, wrap up. We're going home." As fast as I could, I wrapped up his welding cables, and we rushed into town to grab our bags. It was nothing but rock and roll music the whole ride home at over 130 kilometers an hour.

When Don dropped me off at home, my father had just arrived back from a job. He and Don chatted for a few minutes but Don was understandably eager to go. My father loved Don like a son, and was so proud of him for having a child and starting a family. He would have loved to celebrate with Don that day but was clearly unable to. So when we got in the house, he asked me to pour him a celebratory drink. His face gleamed with pride as he sipped his whiskey and spoke of Don's new family.

The next couple of weeks on the farm ran fairly smoothly. My father didn't yell as much, and he showed me more and more respect. It felt really nice. I was reminded of how he was such a cool guy when he wasn't mad, and I was excited to start building a better friendship with him. He had work lined up for us—a pipeline job that would allow us to be home every night and that would last the whole winter. We talked about it briefly and decided that I would quit working for Don and become my father's helper. I was going to start my apprenticeship under him and become a welder just like him. The job was to start at the beginning of December.

My father had a dream of us working together on the pipeline, and that I would then buy the neighbours' farm so we could farm together too. This was his dream, not mine. My parents never asked me what my dreams were, and I didn't want to upset them, so I kept my mouth shut and went along for the ride.

Chapter 3

Answering Questions

It was getting late, nearly ten o'clock at night, and still there was no word from my father. The police didn't have any news for us either and were starting to send people home. I knew they wouldn't find anything. I had scoured every crevice of our property already, and no one knew our land like I did. They had searched our sheds, shops, and barns with dogs. It dawned on me at one point that I had missed one place while looking for him—the hopper in our combine. When I told the officer, he replied that his fellow officers would look into it for me.

As the neighbours filed out the door, one of the police officers asked my mother and me if we would come into Wetaskiwin to answer some questions. We agreed. I thought we would discuss a search plan for the next day, and possibly compile a list of suspects if there was any hint of foul play. A weird thought entered my mind. *What if the police search our house?* My bedroom was full of stolen stereo equipment. I also had a switchblade in my room that

I was fairly certain was illegal in Canada. I got that sinking feeling again. *My dad's missing person report could land me in jail for possession of stolen property and an illegal weapon.* Thinking on my feet, I told the officer I had to run downstairs to grab my wallet.

My mind raced as I ran downstairs. I quickly decided there was nothing I could do. There was just too much merchandise. I grabbed my wallet and the switchblade, which I slipped into my front pocket. It was one less thing for which they could charge me. I came to terms with the fact that they would find the stereo equipment and I would be charged with possession of stolen property. Up the stairs I went to the landing at the front door.

The police officer said, "Scott, it's protocol. We have to search you before you get into the cruiser."

Trying to keep my cool, I had only one word ringing through my head: *FUCK!* I looked at my grandmother, then at my aunts. What would they think when they saw I had an illegal weapon on me? A female officer searched me. She grabbed the back pockets of my jeans and ran her hands down the backs of my legs. Then, working her way back up from my feet, she patted down the fronts of my legs. As she reached my front pockets, I shifted my body and she completely missed the knife. *Phew. Dodged a bullet there.* Surprisingly, nobody in the room noticed she had missed my front pockets. They searched my mother and removed a pocketknife they found in her purse. We then arranged to meet my grandparents after we were done at the police station.

They loaded my mother and me into an unmarked cruiser. *If I were a real criminal, I could stab the driver and run away*, I thought. I looked at my mother. She looked sick. Her skin was pale and her eyes empty.

I broke the silence between us.

"What kind of questions do you think they're gonna ask us that we haven't already answered?"

"I don't know, Scott."

"Did you see which field he went in when he left?"

"No, I didn't."

Does he have any enemies? I thought. *Has he shown any signs of wanting to bail on us? Where would he go if he left us?*

The rest of the trip into town was graveyard silent—the kind of silence that leaves a disturbing feeling in your bones and sends a shiver down your spine.

At the police station, the officers walked us through the back doors, escorted me to the front lobby, and asked me to remain seated until they needed me. They kept my mother in the back and asked her questions first.

The waiting room was dark. The police station was closed, so the lights were off and the room had a gloomy feel. Crime posters covered the concrete walls. One lonely plant sat in the corner to my left and looked as if it were jailed there for life. The hard plastic chairs were uncomfortable and bolted to the floor, and there was no reading material to keep me occupied while I waited. I sat patiently for one hour, then restlessly for another. I couldn't keep my eyes open, yet I couldn't sleep. I was starting to get annoyed. Eventually I had to pee so badly I started banging on the bulletproof glass that separated the receptionist's area from the public, hoping someone would hear and let me use the facilities. The glass had no give though and didn't make much sound, so I sat back down. Finally, I saw someone walking behind the glass.

I quickly jumped out of my chair and yelled through the small opening in the glass, "Hey, I need to use the washroom! I gotta take a piss!"

"I'll send someone to come get you in a bit." The officer shouted as he walked off.

What a fucking joke this place is. I'm ready to piss my pants. I looked at the plant and thought about pissing in it. It was a good ten minutes that I'd been staring at it before an officer came into the room.

"We're ready for you, Scott," he said firmly, as though I were a patient in a doctor's office.

Irritated, I replied, "I have to go to the washroom first. I've been holding it for like an hour." He walked me there—four concrete walls and a toilet big enough for the Jolly Green Giant. The whole place was depressing.

Feeling empty and energized, I walked out of the bathroom ready to answer questions and find my father. My surge in energy surprised me because it must have been one or two in the morning. The officer led me into a room with a desk, a couple of chairs, and a tape recorder. A female officer was in the room as well. As I sat down, she told me they had to tape our conversation as part of a new, province-wide policy. I didn't care—I just wanted to get to it. They started by asking me to describe in detail what I had done that day, and then asked me some basic questions about my parents. Had they been fighting that morning? I told them that everything was fine, and that I couldn't see any reason why my dad would be missing.

"My father and I were planning on going to a job together very soon, in about a week." Shaking my head, I continued. "This disappearance is just out of character for him. Something's not right."

"How was your parents' relationship? Was there any abuse?"

"Their relationship was good. There wasn't any abuse."

"So you're telling us your parents didn't fight?"

"Well of course they fought, but it was pretty normal. It's not like my father went around beating my mom."

"Well, did he hit her?"

"Not that I ever saw." The lies flowed easily. My father had always taught us to protect each other. "I've seen my dad push my mom a couple of times, but he never beat her down."

What do these questions have to do with my missing father? I wondered. The more questions I was asked, the more aggravated I grew. It seemed as if they were moving off topic and not concentrating on the task at hand.

"Did your father ever hit you?" they asked.

"No."

"So you're telling us your father never spanked you."

"Well obviously he spanked me when I did wrong, but he never went around hitting me for no reason."

"Then tell us, what was your relationship like with your father?"

"It was good. We worked together, fished together, hunted together. Everything was normal." I was doing what I had been taught—to never rat anyone out, especially family. I knew these people had no clue what happened behind closed doors on the farm, and I didn't want them to know. It was embarrassing, and at the time I felt it was irrelevant.

They focused their eyes on mine and asked again, "Scott, was your father abusive?"

"I just told you, no." I was a vault, locked up tight, not wanting my father to be charged with abuse and put in jail. No incriminating evidence about my family was getting out. I wanted to concentrate on locating my father—find clues and crack the code to his disappearance. I sure as hell didn't want to be sitting in the police station answering stupid questions. But they kept pressing on and on with the petty shit.

Then it came. After close to an hour of interrogation, I was asked the first question that got my mind working overtime. The male police officer asked me with a straight face, "How can you just sit there after loading your father's body into the tractor bucket?"

"What?"

The officer repeated the question.

Totally taken off guard, I sat up in my chair. "I have no clue what you're talking about."

They stopped the tape and left the room. *What the hell was that about?* While I pondered the situation, I played with the switch-blade that was now in my coat pocket.

When the two officers came back, they had more questions—detailed ones. What time had I left for town? When was I in the dealership? When did I get home? They wanted me to put exact times on everything I had done that day. Approximately ten-thirty was not acceptable. Was it 10:26 or was it 10:27? This was almost impossible for me to say, but I was under a lot of pressure, so I did the best I could with my mind running in so many directions. I was drained and baffled.

And then the male cop asked me, "Did you need help when you dragged your father's dead body through the house?"

What? "I have no clue what you're talking about."

Suddenly, in complete disbelief, I realized that my father had to be dead. Yet somehow, it didn't hit me or affect me at the time…I guess because I was being bombarded with so many questions and accusations. I was in shock, yet in survival mode.

The probing continued. Repeatedly they asked me how I could sit there with a cold look on my face after I had dragged my father's body through the house and into the tractor bucket.

I slowly sank lower in my chair, trying to hide. My answer was the same every time.

"I have no clue what you're talking about."

The female cop asked questions pertaining to my feelings, and the male cop asked me about the facts. The more questions they asked, the more I was able to piece together what had happened to my father. To this day, no one has ever said to me, "Scott, your father has passed away."

My back was against the wall and I had no way out. There's no way to describe my feelings in that moment—too many emotions rushed through my body. I was so confused and had no clue what to do.

Children are taught to trust the police. But what if the police are your enemies? Then to whom do you turn? I had been taught to tell my father if I ever had a problem I thought I couldn't solve or handle. He would know what to do in any situation. Like Superman, he would save me.

But my father was dead, so I had no one to turn to. The police were accusing me of things I hadn't done, and I had no father to save me. I felt like an animal in a trap. Morning was approaching and I was crashing—sinking into a hole. The more questions they asked me, the more I hated the police.

The examination got more direct with their accusations geared towards me. As it went on the police became more and more abusive. I knew something bad was about to come out of their mouths because they would turn the tape recorder off. With the recorder on they would ask me questions such as, "So tell us again what time you got home from Ponoka?" I would respond and then the male officer would turn the tape recorder off and yell something like, "You loaded your fucking dad into a tractor bucket and dumped his body into a dead animal pit you lying piece of shit!"

The female officer would chime in "How can you sit there and not shed a tear right after you murdered your father?"

Screamed at for hours. I was a wounded animal; scared but ready to strike. The tension was tight and about to snap. Clenching the switchblade in my hand, I thought about doing something I would regret, hoping it would get me out of this mess.

"Fuck you! I have no clue what the fuck you're talking about! I was the one looking for my dad all day. No one else. Do you think I would waste my time searching for him if I knew where he was? I'm fucking sick of this shit and your fucking accusations!"

It was a bad scene. Everyone involved wanted answers and didn't have them. Everyone involved was agitated and growing more impatient. The cops once again walked out of the room then moments later came back. Tempers had cooled a little. Or at least I thought they had. I was slouched in my chair with my ass barely on the seat. My hat was pulled down so my eyes were slightly visible.

"Why don't you come clean and tell us what you did today," the female cop asked calmly.

I looked up at her and quietly said, "I already did."

"You murdering piece of shit!" she suddenly screamed at the top of her lungs. "Sit up in your chair when I'm talking to you." Rushing at me, she punched me square in the forehead, knocking my head back and causing my hat to fly off.

Without thinking, I reacted. I jumped out of my chair and grabbed her by the throat with my left hand while my right hand stayed in my pocket, on my switchblade. Our eyes locked as I slammed her against the door, and even though she was unaware of the potential danger in my pocket, I could see she was scared. Her partner grabbed me and threw me back. She tried rushing me again but he held her off. They left the room again and let me cool down.

The same shit continued for another hour. They walked in and out of the interrogation room playing good cop/bad cop.

"Would you be willing to take a lie detector test?"

"No."

"Why not?"

"Well it's a machine I know nothing about. I don't trust machines I'm not familiar with. I'm not gonna place my life in the hands of something I don't trust." My response seemed logical to me. I was also worried about the questions they would ask. What if they inquired about the abuse within the family?

I was starting to understand that I was being accused of murder. The thought scared me, but during those early hours of the morning, I just wanted it all to be over. I now understand how cops can get people to admit to crimes they didn't commit. They spent hour after hour accusing me of the same thing over and over again. This is a form of torture in itself. At this point, I had said everything but "I killed him," and I was considering saying it just to stop the torture.

It was now around seven o'clock in the morning and I had been awake for twenty-four hours. It was the first time in my life I had ever been awake for so long. I could barely keep my eyes open. A bed in a jail cell was actually looking good at this point. My mind was mangled and blank. I can't remember the details—how many times I was asked a certain question, or how many times I was screamed at or slapped. The cops chopped at me, but they still couldn't break me down. I had been trained to endure this pain from years of abuse. My father had slapped me around and punched me a lot worse than this. He had also called me worse names and yelled at me more than they ever could have. I was a wall unwilling to fall. But the worst was to come—they had an ace up their sleeve.

The two cops I had grown to hate grabbed me and told me to come with them. Each held one of my arms firmly. I was defeated. There was no fight left in me. *Just give me a jail cell and let's call it a night.*

They sat me down at a table out in the open, in front of all the other cops. I felt as if I were a freak on display for everyone to see. A well-dressed man in a crisp, white dress shirt and creased dress pants walked into the room. I could tell he was a cop of some kind in civilian clothing. I sensed he was dangerous. It was like a scene from those cop movies where you just know which one is the boss, and the most badass cop. He was it. He had a swagger of confidence. His square chin and strong, rugged face meant business. He walked up to me and introduced himself—a detective brought in from Red Deer to interrogate me. For a minute, he stared me down, sizing up his opponent.

No words were spoken as he nonchalantly threw two pictures on the table in front of me. Sensing that the pictures were of something I didn't want to see, I looked away. Calmly, he told me to look at them. All the other officers watched eagerly, as if they were back in university wanting to learn something.

He's the professor, they're the students, and I'm just a prop.

He leaned into me and told me again to look at the pictures. I whimpered, "No." Deep inside, I knew these pictures were of my father's body. I didn't want to see my father dead. With a deep breath to calm myself, I closed my eyes.

In one swift motion, the detective backhanded my hat off and grabbed a handful of my hair. Jerking my head back, he leaned in close to me and whispered in my ear, "I told you to look at the pictures."

My entire body was so numb I couldn't feel the pain of my hair being pulled from my skull.

Gradually, I opened my eyes and stared at him. My voice was trembling, and my jaw shook. "I don't want to look at the pictures." As slow as the sun goes down, I closed my eyes again, and took a sluggish deep breath. Then an unexplainable tranquility entered my body, as if I had made peace with God.

The investigator let go of my hair.

"Why won't you look at the fucking pictures?"

"I don't wanna have nightmares for the rest of my life because of some photos you made me look at."

"Are you scared of what you will see?

Under my breath, I replied, "Yes."

He shouted at me like a sergeant in the army trying to motivate his troops. "Look at the goddamn pictures! Look at what you've done!"

Eyes closed, I blocked out everyone in the room and sat in the silence of my mind. There was a slight pause, and then the investigator grabbed the hair on the back of my head again. "I told you to look at the fucking photos!" His bottomless voice made the hair on my neck stand as he forced my face directly at the pictures. My eyes were now clenched shut. In a quick motion, the investigator slammed my face into the table, smashing my nose into my skull. I opened my eyes and had a second to glance at the pictures before the investigator lifted my head off the table and slammed my face once again into the hard wooden surface. This time I dipped my chin so my forehead hit the table, and a loud bang echoed in the room. Pulling my hair tightly with both hands, the investigator held my head six inches from the photos. With watering eyes, I finally took a long look at what I didn't want to see.

I can't remember any sounds or any actions. I can't remember the feeling of my hair being ripped from my scalp. I just remember the images slowly chiselling themselves into my brain. I was hollow with no feeling as my father's lifeless, naked body lying in the dead animal pit registered. It looked so pale and cold. He lay there on his back, facing me, with no expression. I felt so helpless. I wanted to reach out and save him. No breath entered my body and my mouth dried up. I had tasted death for the first time.

The investigator let go of my head. I lifted it up, almost dizzy. There was no life left in me. The grim reaper had taken my soul. I looked right through the officers as if they were nonexistent. Everything seemed one-dimensional.

The investigator lightly slapped my face. "Hey!" he yelled to break me out of my trance. I looked up at him. "Do you have anything to tell me?"

I could barely reply. "No."

"Are you ready to go to jail?"

I swallowed what felt like a dry hairball in my mouth. "Yes."

"Are you confessing to murder?"

I shook my head. "Nope." I took a deep breath and spoke up louder, and more firmly. "I just want all of this to be over. Charge me with murder, put me in jail, and I will beat your fucking ass in court."

He shouted to the other officers while waving them over.

"Book him!"

Exhausted and beaten down, I didn't care.

An officer stepped up to me and barked out, "Scott Leonard Hay, you are being charged with accessory to murder." He followed up by reading me my rights.

I didn't hear them. I didn't hear anything. I didn't care. I only wanted to lay my head down and sleep. I was just an eighteen-year-old kid who lived with his parents. I had no idea how much trouble I was in.

Chapter 4

My Mother

My mother was born in Edmonton, Alberta, and raised in a village near Pigeon Lake. I was told her father was a respectable man who died when she was very young. They say he fell down the stairs and shot himself during the fall. Plenty of speculation and rumours surround this story. Many years later, my grandmother remarried a man named Carl. Carl was a funny man whom I knew as Grandpa. He would always hide around corners and jump out and scare me. When I was five, Carl committed suicide. They found him hanging in the garage.

At the age of fifteen, my mother started dating my father, a farm boy. She had no vehicle, so most of her time was spent on my dad's farm with his family. This worked well because my father had an older sister and a younger sister for my mom to befriend while he was working in the fields. The girls got along great and had fun working and partying together. My grandmother taught my mom how to work, and she proved to be an excellent student.

It wasn't long until she was cooking, cleaning, gardening, and sewing on a regular basis, quickly transforming into a farm girl. My father came from a very close family, and my mother quickly became part of it. She wasn't just my father's girlfriend—she was a sister and daughter to the rest of the family.

My mother became pregnant with Mike when she was just seventeen years old. The next few months proved to be a busy time for her. She turned eighteen in April, finished school in June (one course short of graduating), got married in a shotgun wedding on June 25, 1976, and in October had her first child.

She was a very hard worker. She would feed us boys while washing the family's clothing, and making a dress for my cousin at the same time. Once we moved to the farm, my mother took her work ethic to a whole new level. She still did everything she had done before, but now she was also in charge of taking care of the cows and horses, and tending to the fields. She learned to drive a tractor, assist a cow with the birth of a calf, shoot a gun, and even butcher pigs, cows, and chickens. My mother was a smart lady and learned quickly.

I remember her being an excellent seamstress. When I was in grade five she made me this amazing Tweety Bird costume. I was so proud of it because most of my classmates' costumes were made of plastic and mine was a one-piece, furry costume with padding that turned my skinny body into this fluffy little yellow bird. She also made a lot of western-style button-up shirts that were quite stylish, and when I bought a dirt bike she even made me special motocross pants. Her specialty though was dresses. She would make my sister and cousin exquisite, princess-like dresses, puffed out on the bottom and form fitting on top. I hated it when she would make my cousin dresses because my cousin and I were the same size, so I would have to wear the dress while my mother fitted it. Of course my mother had to take pictures of me wearing the dresses to show family and friends. I was mortified whenever she did.

She was a very sociable person and got along with everyone. She stayed away from confrontation and was always easy to please. Everyone liked her, and neighbours would often come over for coffee or tea. Once in a while, if the mood was right, my mother would drink with her friends. She didn't drink much though, because she would get violently ill the next day. Needless to say, with three children to take care of, she didn't party very much. She did like to curl, and was excellent at the sport. In no time, she worked her way up from lead to skip, and proved she deserved to be there by winning a few bonspiels. In the winters she would travel to local communities for bonspiels, and we children loved tagging along so we could play with the other children.

My mother always provided for us and was always there for us. If we wanted to play a game, she would finish her chores quickly so she could take time to play with us. If we ever had a request for lunch or dinner, she made it for us. If one of us was in trouble with our father and it started getting out of hand, she often stepped in for us.

Through my father's family she became involved in the church, and she practiced her faith without question. She studied and taught Bible lessons, and was involved in Sunday school and Vacation Bible School. She took us to church frequently and when we were old enough, made sure we went if she was unable to go. She learned most of her morals and family values from my father's family. Her own family seemed uncaring, almost nonexistent.

My mother and my father were married for twenty-one years, and they loved each other dearly. I remember them cuddling on the couch and watching movies like high school kids. They did everything together, from going to town to going for walks. As a team, they cared for and raised their three children. For birthdays and anniversaries they bought each other gifts, and when my father was out of town, he called my mother every night to talk. And their sex life was never dead. I would often cover my head with a pillow or go outside because I heard "noises" coming from their room.

Though they were very much in love, it goes without saying that their relationship had turmoil. They fought, and those fights could get ugly. Screaming and yelling often led to pushing and sometimes hitting. It was always my father who got physical. I remember him throwing my mother on the ground or smacking her on the side of the head. When they fought at night, my siblings and I just lay in our beds—scared. The yelling and the screaming chilled us to the bone. I remember being frozen with fear listening to my father's rough voice and my mother's cries, hearing the loud crashes and bangs—sounds that led me to believe my mother was being thrown around. My senses sharpened and in the darkness with my eyes wide open I lay there, fearing the worst. But when I woke up, everything was fine.

They forgave each other easily and quickly. I usually didn't know what their fights were about, but when I got older I started to understand some of them. They fought over petty little things and got carried away. For example, we lived thirty minutes from town, so we would get groceries once a week. If my mother forgot to get milk or cigarettes, a fight would spark, my mother would roll her eyes, and my father would fly into a fiery rage.

When I was seventeen, my mother left my father. She had it all planned out in advance. During the days, my father was working a pipeline job about an hour from our farm. One day, my mother packed up all her things and picked up my sister at the elementary school. She then drove to the high school and had me paged to the parking lot. When I walked outside I saw the car loaded to the roof with her stuff. She wanted me to go with her, but I wouldn't.

"Mom, we can go back to the farm and unpack everything. Nobody has to know that you were gonna do this."

"Scott, I can't keep living my life this way," she replied, tears running down her face. "I have to go. I have to move on. Please, Scott, just come with me."

"Fuck, Mom, how are you gonna survive? Where are you gonna get money from?"

"I've taken a little bit from your father—enough to last me a month. Obviously I'll have to get a job."

"Mom, I'd love to come, but logically it's not the best decision for me."

"I understand. It's your decision. But just know that I love you and want you to be with me. Scott, I really gotta go."

In disbelief, after a quick hug with my sister, I watched my mom drive away.

I knew staying with my father would mean an ass-kicking here or there, but I still loved him. Plus, I knew that he was planning on buying me a new truck, and I wouldn't get that from my mother. At seventeen, every kid dreams of having his own vehicle. I also didn't want to move away from the area I had grown up in my whole life. I cherished my friends and loved my family members, and they were all in the Wetaskiwin area. Red Deer was an hour away, and it seemed much too far at the time.

Worried about what my father would do when he got home from work, I called my grandparents and aunties and asked them to come over, knowing that if there were a lot of people around, my father would probably keep his cool. When my father got out of the truck he was smiling and happy to see everyone, but as soon as he saw our faces, he knew something was wrong. We told him my mother had left him and taken his little princess. Expecting the worst, I was blown away when he shrugged it off and said, "Well let's have a drink." He sat down at our table, and I poured him a rye and coke. Everything seemed okay. He talked, and laughed, and drank with the family all night.

The next morning he quit his job, and to my excitement, while we fed the cows, he spoke about selling the farm. He also expressed concern about my mom's and sister's safety but remained calm. My mother had said she would phone Mike on Sunday, as Mike was living in Red Deer, so on Sunday morning my father and I drove to Mike's place. My dad wanted to talk to her to see if everything was all right, and to make sure she and my sister were safe. We waited all day, but she never called.

The next day at school, I was fairly upbeat about the breakup because it was looking like my father would sell the farm. From my point of view, the farm was the root of most of our problems. But I arrived home that afternoon to find my mother was back. Everyone acted like nothing had happened…as usual. We were laughing like the Cosbys in no time.

I never found out why my mother came back. Michelle told me Dad had shown up at their new place with a gun and made them move back. But she never actually saw a gun, and I just couldn't imagine my father doing that. And if he had, why hadn't my mom phoned the police? Or talked to someone about the problem? I never understood it. And I never will. I realize now that the truth is, you can never understand what drives another until you stand in his or her exact shoes.

Chapter 5

The Confession

I sat in a room full of police officers, awaiting my destiny, which at this point appeared to be a jail cell. The room was buzzing. More people kept showing up, and no one was leaving. I could hear all sorts of chatter but nothing of any importance to me. Every few minutes I felt a small burst of energy and thought about how I wanted to take a flame-thrower to this depressing shithole they called a police station. After nine hours of abuse, I also wanted the officers to be in the police station when I torched it. I was angry. I was pissed off. I needed to sleep.

Then, over all of the useless chatter, I heard a man yell out as if he had gotten a bingo: "She confessed!" I looked at him as he walked directly towards me.

The officer standing guard by my side was clueless.

"What?" he asked.

"She just confessed, but she wants to see the boy."

In the background, I heard everyone talking excitedly about my mother's confession. The officer beside me shook my chair and ordered me to stand up. I was sick of being treated this way, so I paused for a moment. It was my only way of rebelling. "I told you to stand up!" the officer bellowed, and shook my chair again. I stood up with my hands in my pockets. My right hand was on the switchblade, my thumb on the trigger. I looked at the officer and smirked as I thought about stabbing him in the throat. I never would have done it, but knowing I had the opportunity to capitalize on the officers' mistake, brought me a little comfort. He escorted me to the small interrogation room.

My mother was a mess. She had aged overnight. Her face was wet from tears and her eyes swollen from crying. She reached out and pulled me in. "Scott!" She said my name as though we hadn't seen each other in ten years. As she squeezed me tightly, she tried to muddle out some words, but all I could make out was, "I'm sorry." The officer closed the door as he left the room. My mother let me go, but I could still feel her desperate grasp.

I sat facing her, facing a murderer.

She trembled uncontrollably and instantly started to rant, trying to justify her actions—trying to give me some good reason why she had killed my father. She told me about the abuse she had endured in the relationship, and that she couldn't take it anymore. To an extent, I could relate. In some sort of way, I understood. Then she took me off guard. She told me my father had been with other women, and that she had been there when he was with them. She would stand guard to ensure us kids never came around. None of this made sense to me. It couldn't have happened under the roof of my own home without my knowing about it. I would have seen the signs: shoes at the door, a car parked in the driveway, or even a phone call from an unknown number. This was way too much for me to process at the time.

My mother was panicking, desperately wanting my acceptance. She was reaching out to me and wanting me to tell her it was okay.

"What happened?" was all I could say.

"Well Scott, after I made you guys breakfast and you went to Ponoka, your father and I got ready to go to Wetaskiwin. Your dad asked me about how much money was in the bank account because he wanted to pay back money he had borrowed from your grandparents. I told him we didn't have enough to pay them back.

"Your dad got mad at me because he didn't understand why he didn't have enough money. He'd just finished that job and felt he should have had enough to pay them back.

"We were in the bedroom and he started throwing me around and hitting me. I was just so sick of this shit, Scott. I was fed up with being treated this way and living life this way. Your dad ran a bath, and while he did, I went downstairs and grabbed the Remington 243.

"I only put one bullet in it. Then I grabbed the big butchering knife out of the storage room and went back upstairs. The bath-room door was partly open, and your father was asleep in the tub. I poked the gun through the door jamb, and took aim, and shot him in the side of the chest." She trembled with every word.

"Then I grabbed the knife and slit his throat to bleed him out. I had laid some plastic out by the tub, and I wrapped his body in it and then loaded it into the tractor bucket. Finally I drove out to the dead animal pit and put two round straw bales on him so no one would find him.

"Scott, please forgive me. I'm sorry. I'm so, so sorry." Tears raced down her cheeks, and I reassured her that everything would be okay. I could see the pain in her eyes. She was scared—scared she would lose her children, scared she had lost her life. The room was heavy. The air was hard to breathe. It felt like goodbye.

A few moments later, we were interrupted by an officer. We had been given only a couple of minutes to talk. Under the circumstances, it was clearly not enough time. This time though, when the officer opened the door, I could see he felt some compassion. He calmly said, "We have to go, Scott." Anyone who walked into that room would have felt the pain, the stress.

As I stood, my mother jumped up and reached out to me one last time. Her hands clenched my shoulders, and I could feel the tips of her fingers dig into my arms as she pulled me close and squeezed me with all her might. I knew she wouldn't let go. She buried her face in my neck, and I felt her tears running down onto my shoulders. My family doesn't hug. It felt as though my mother were making up for all the years of not showing affection. Would it be the last time she would ever hug me or see me?

The unknown can be terrifying. It can take your breath away. It can be like thinking you saw a ghost and not wanting to believe it. The officer leaned in and tapped me on the shoulder. My mother and I didn't let go, and like a boxing referee, he was forced to split us up. My mother was shaking so much she could hardly sit down again. I thought she was going to collapse. As I walked out, I glanced back and heard the desperation in her voice. "I love you, Scott."

I was immediately escorted outside and into a police cruiser. The sun was rising on that snowless December day. I stared out the window as I leaned my head against it. The world passed me by as my life stood still. No snow, no flowers, no leaves on the trees. The grass was all dead. I felt dead.

The cruiser pulled up to my grandparents' house, and the officer walked me to the front door. My dad's brother opened the door, and the officer followed me inside, where I removed my cowboy boots and hung up my Carhartt jacket.

Patting my shoulder, my uncle said, "You don't have to explain anything, Scott. The cops were here earlier tonight and told us what happened to your father. How you holdin' up?"

I was fed up with questions. "I'm tired."

"You can go sleep in the basement."

While I walked down the hall I heard the officer talking to my uncle. I slowed my pace so I could hear what they were saying.

"Keep an eye on Scott. We were pretty hard on him tonight."

As I heard the front door close, I walked down the stairs. My uncle was right behind me. I couldn't stand any more, and plopped down on the edge of the bed. My eyes were just slits.

My uncle sat down beside me.

"What happened?"

I was too tired to go over the whole ordeal, so I tried to keep it brief. I told him about being questioned all night about little details such as time and distance. I told him that they had charged me, and that was why my mother had confessed.

"What did the cop mean when he told me they were hard on you?"

"Ah, they yelled at me quite a bit and smacked me around a little."

"What did your mom have to say?"

I told him the story of the murder and about some of the stories my mom had told me about my father being with other women and abusing her. At this point I was a zombie and my uncle could see that, so he let me go to sleep.

I slept the day away. When I woke at four in the afternoon, I couldn't believe it. I had never slept that late in my life, but I had never been awake for twenty-six hours straight before either. I heard people upstairs—not just family, but friends of the family too. I groaned, not wanting to face everyone and answer questions all day, again. Still in shock, I just wanted to be alone and watch television. As I slowly walked upstairs, I hoped my sluggish pace would give people time to leave. I opened the door and immediately heard, "Scott must be up."

It was as though they were all waiting for me so I could answer their questions. The kitchen was full of food. Everyone greeted me and asked how I was doing. "I'm fine," was my robotic response. I grabbed some finger food and looked around. The house was already filling up with flowers, cards, and food. My cousins were watching television, and during a commercial break I heard my life make "breaking news." I paid no attention. Friends and family continued the grilling that had started at the police station. "What time did you leave to Ponoka? What time did you come home? Were your parents fighting when you left? Didn't something seem wrong when you came home from Ponoka?"

I ducked out every chance I got, to try to unwind, but it was hard to get away from the commotion. People kept coming over to pay their respects. The phone rang off the hook. Then the broadcaster began the six o'clock news with his hottest story of the day: Bruce Hay's murder. His spiel ended with, "Scott Hay is currently being held in police custody for the murder of his father."

I got a small chuckle out of that. *Here I am sitting at my grandparents' house, and our nation thinks I'm a murderer. What a joke.* The media spreads so many lies—if a person wanted real answers, he would have a better chance getting them from the *National Enquirer.* My uncle got on the phone and told the news station that I was not in police custody and was in fact sitting with him at my grandparent's house.

When the station attempted to solicit him for more information, he told them where they could stick it and that they needed to set the record straight. Later on that night, during a sitcom commercial break, a split-second announcement came on. "We have a correction to a statement from earlier in our broadcast. Scott Hay is no longer in custody for the murder of his father."

That's it? The broadcaster's words had practically been cut off by the commercial. No one would have heard it. *Everyone is still going to think I'm a killer. Oh well, who fucking cares?* I knew my life had far worse complications at the moment. I didn't need to worry myself about what other people were assuming.

I fought to stay awake to watch the eleven o'clock news, thinking that my name would be cleared. Boy was I wrong. There was a small segment on my father's death and no mention of the false information about my being in police custody for the murder. It was total bullshit. I felt as if everyone—Canada, the police, friends, and even worse, some of my own family members—were looking at me as though I were a cold-blooded killer. I had had enough; it was late, I was tired, and I was in desperate need of a good night's rest.

It would be at least a week before I got one.

Chapter 6

My Father

Bruce Hay was born in Wetaskiwin in December 1957. From childhood, he always played by his own rules. Passionate about guns and hunting, he was a rough and tough man's man. He enjoyed drinks with friends, smoked a pack a day, and never backed down from a fight, but he also loved to learn and read. Though a welder by trade, his heart was in farming.

Despite my father's many flaws, his good qualities still remain unmatched in my mind. He always believed family should come first, and he wouldn't hesitate to give of himself for his family. He looked up to his father and would always tell us kids about our strong and hard-working grandfather. My grandfather was well respected in the community because of his gentle demeanour, yet he was known to be strong as an ox.

My father Bruce Hay was also a great friend to many people, and he enjoyed helping those he cared about. He was a grooms-man in seven weddings—an indication of the kind of friend he was. When he and his friends got together, usually once a week, they would tell stories of the "old days" and drink a bottle of whisky. Royal Reserve was their standard choice, but the Crown Royal came out for special occasions. My father was always looking for a good time, and was generally the one to bring that good time to the party. He had a great sense of humour and was always joking around. And no matter how much he drank, he was up early, ready to work.

Though he loved his friends he spent most of his spare time with his boys, teaching us how to fish, how to hunt, how to build things, and most of all, how to have fun. He had a playful nature and loved kids. My father often took my brother and me down to Mount Red Park to go fishing. He packed us each a bag of Hawkins Cheezies and a can of Pepsi and set us up with a bobber and a hook with a worm on it. We sat for hours talking and making jokes. At home, he taught us how to clean our fish, and then my mother cooked our catches for dinner. These memories of my family are some of the pleasant ones that will stick in my mind forever.

My father's passion for hunting was a little odd because my grandfather didn't hunt much in his lifetime. Actually, no one in my family ever hunted, so my father was forced to teach himself. He read books and magazines—whatever he could—to learn more about it. This passion became a part-time job in the early 'eighties when there was little to no work in the oil patch. Despite the recession, fur prices were high. My father had a real trap line, and in the mornings he took the snowmobile down to the creek to check all of his muskrat and beaver traps. Then he picked me up and we drove his truck around to check his coyote traps and snares. While we drove, we scanned the earth like hawks for anything that moved. Anyone who knew my father knew that if he pulled the gun off the seat to shoot something, it was as good as dead. He was an amazing shot and had no problem challenging anyone to a shooting contest.

One year, we had a cow with a broken leg lying out in our field, waiting to die. Since it was cruel to let her suffer, my father decided to shoot her. He told me to go the basement, where he kept his guns, and to bring him his Remington 243. That was his first and favourite rifle, the pride of the fleet and the rifle with which he killed everything when he started hunting. He and that gun had a bond of sorts that I can't explain. It seemed to be an extension of his body. When I came up the stairs with the gun, my father said to me, "Twenty bucks says I can kill her from here." I chuckled to myself. I knew he was good, but this cow was approximately four hundred yards out in the field. It wasn't a clear shot either. My father would have to shoot through a small bush, and most of the cow's body was hidden in a large divot in the land. So I took the bet, thinking my father's cockiness would bite him in the ass. Acting as if the cow were fifty feet from him, he walked outside, leaned on a power pole, and without any hesitation pulled the trigger.

"Scott, take the quad out to the field to see if she's dead."

That poor cow is going to be in pain, I thought. As I approached her, I wondered where the bullet had gone. Over? Under? In her side? I pulled up, uneasy about what I would find. To my greatest amazement, my father had shot the cow perfectly between the eyes. I welched on the bet, but will never forget the shot and how he took it with such confidence. My father was wired to be a skilful fighter and hunter. He should have been a soldier.

Bruce Hay was a hard, knowledgeable worker and never stopped until the job was done. He acquired his B pressure welding ticket in 1980 and often practiced welding pipe at home. When my brother and I were young, we would have to peel the coating off the pipe my father brought home from work. We spent what seemed like all day doing it, though it was probably only an hour.

When you're four years old, work always seems to take forever to complete. When we were finished peeling the coating off, my father cut the pipe up into many small pieces just to weld it back together for practice. His firm belief in 'practice makes perfect' is what made him a good welder. He earned a good name for himself in the oil patch, where he made a lot of friends. The patch could be slow, but if my father wanted work he would just make a few calls and have a job within a week or two. This was unusual at the time. He was a typical pipeliner—he worked long, hard hours, partied hard, and 'drove it like he stole it.'

One of my first pipeline jobs was a Local 488 union job. I hadn't been out there long when I discovered that my father was fairly well known. Whenever I introduced myself, people would ask, "Are you related to Bruce Hay?" He was respected on the pipeline, and I heard several stories about him in the short time I was out there.

While I was sitting in a bar one night, an old friend of my father's, Rick, told me about how years ago, he had been about to get fired for messing up too many welds. My father caught wind of this and made his way over to Rick's truck to help him. Rick was a rookie at the time and hadn't learned the tricks of the trade. My father, being the generous, helpful man he was, took it upon himself to give the young lad some pointers, and he became a mentor to him. Rick credited my father with saving his job and said he would forever be grateful.

My father wasn't just a smart worker—he was also a "book smart" man who was good at problem solving and excellent when it came to world history. Both my father and my mother were always there to lend a helping hand when I had homework questions. If it was English or science, I asked my mother. If it was mathematics or history, I would ask my father.

Through our father, my brother and I learned skills that many people in this world will never have and that I've always assumed were common sense. For example, he taught us how to skin and butcher an animal, and we even had our own little butcher shop, where we cut and wrapped all of our own meat. We also made our own sausage. Mixing the spices and meat and then putting everything in sausage casings was quite a task. Then we would smoke the sausage in a smokehouse. Learning all these skills was a fun process, and my father was a great teacher.

My dad took pride in raising his two boys and spent a lot of time teaching us how to be "men." Opening doors for our elders, taking your hat off at the dinner table, and saying please and thank you, were just some of the manners that were planted in us. We were his seeds and he wanted us to grow and be independent. I learned to drive our lawnmower when I was four. Soon after, I was riding a dirt bike, and I spent many years on our three-wheeled ATV. By the time I reached the tender age of twelve I was driving vehicles. If my parents slept in on a Sunday and told my sister and me to go to church, I would help Michelle get ready and drive us. It seemed like a small task at the time, but it taught me about independence and responsibility. As a young man, I was able to take on jobs with confidence, and if something seemed out of reach, my father taught me how to reach it.

Only a couple of years after I was able to walk, Mike and I were hauling wood to the house every day as a chore. Though it was hard work, I'm grateful for this experience now because it gave me my work ethic. I remember being seven years old and lying under the truck, where Dad taught us how to change oil and grease the nipples on our vehicles. His lessons were always hands on, which is the best way for anyone to learn a skill. By the time Mike and I were preteens, we were doing oil and lube jobs on all of our family vehicles. My father also taught us street skills. For example, from a young age I was taught to never to tattle. My father hated tattletales. I remember telling on my brother for something, thinking he was going to get a spanking. Instead, I got my ass whooped. At the time, I didn't understand why it was important not to tattle, but now I'm grateful for that life skill.

I was only twelve and Mike fifteen when our father purchased the farm. It was a tough time because it felt like he expected us to already know how to farm. If either of us screwed something up, my father yelled, screamed, and usually smacked us around for a few minutes until he calmed down.

One day we were working on a fence and had to attach cables to pipes using U-bolts. My father had only bought enough U-bolts for the fence we were building that day, but my brother accidentally tightened one so much that it broke off.

"Smarten up and be more careful," my father yelled slapping him on the side of the head. "We don't have any extras."

Instantly the situation was high stress. I knew that from this point on, Mike and I would have to be very attentive to my father's words and body language. The fuse of his anger had been lit, and one more fuckup could set off an explosion. Mike was nineteen at the time and a six-foot-four, two-hundred-and-eighty-pound ogre, that was unsure of his strength.

"Scott, run to the shop and see if you can find another U-bolt this size," my father barked handing me the broken U-bolt.

I immediately did as he asked, and after some searching, found a replacement. "That just saved the day," I said to myself as I rushed back to my father. We continued working, but Mike and I were on pins and needles knowing our dad could lose his cool at any moment. And then . . .

Snap!

I noticed before my father did and stared in disbelief—my brother held another broken bolt in his hand. I knew this was it. Chills ran down my spine as my core temperature rose. I looked at my father and waited for the reaction.

Boom!

Dad exploded. Screaming and yelling, he rushed at my brother like a raging bull. Mike hardly had enough time to stand before my father slapped him hard across the head and threw him to the ground. Grabbing Mike by his hair and throat, he pinned his head against the ground and started kneeing him repeatedly in the skull.

Gritting his teeth my father screamed, "You stupid piece of shit! I told you to be more careful!" My father let go of Mike but continued his rant. Mike's massive body swayed as he stood up. His eyes were glazed over, and he looked punch-drunk. Then my father looked at him and pointed at the house. "Mike, I want you to pack your shit and get the fuck out of here—now!"

"Okay," my brother mumbled. He ran to the house and backed his truck up to the door. My father and I continued working. The air was tight and tense. About ten minutes later, my father began stretching the cable out with the ATV. As he approached the road he looked both ways to ensure no traffic was coming. When he looked left he did a double take.

"Unhook the cable from the quad!" he screamed. I ran up and did as he asked, then looked down the road to see my brother running in the distance. My father raced off on the ATV in pursuit.

I stood on the road watching it all unfold and wondered, *Why didn't Mike take his truck? And why is Dad chasing him?* I was worried for Mike, who had just realized Dad was hot on his tail. He was the 'hunted' and my father was the 'hunter.' My brother was taller than my father and outweighed him by almost one hundred pounds, but my father was stronger, and a veteran fighter.

Escaping the road, my brother jumped a fence and frantically ran for the trees like the many scared coyotes my father had chased in the past. I knew he wouldn't stop running until he was caught. Losing sight of Mike in the trees, my father finally gave up the hunt and began screaming words I couldn't make out.

Mike stayed at his friend's for a week before returning home. He later said that his ears rang for days and his head was bruised and swollen from the beating.

People ask why he came back. In hindsight, I realize that my father hadn't wanted him to leave. He always just reacted in the moment. The truth is, we loved and respected my father and believed he was a good man—he just had this temper that would explode in a split second. As always, Mike quickly forgave my father and acted as though nothing had happened. I realize now that this wasn't the proper way to deal with things, but this was all we knew.

I always understood that my father loved me, but I only remember him telling me so once. I was fifteen years old, and he came downstairs and sat beside me on the couch. As he put his arm around my shoulders, tears slowly filled his eyes. "Scott, I'm sorry for being so hard on you boys. It's hard to understand, but I'm this way because I want you to be the best men you can be. I push you guys hard so when you get to the real world, you won't have any issues with work or other people. You'll be able to hold your heads high, and no one will ever be able to call you lazy or stupid. Someday when you're older, you'll know what I'm talking about and thank me for being hard on you." He bowed his head and started to weep. Then he squeezed me tight and pulled my head against his. A moment later, he lifted his tear-drenched face and looked me right in the eye. "I love you with all my life, Scott. Without question I would die for you, and if God wanted I would live the rest of my life in Hell to give you a better life. I truly mean it." For a moment we stared at each other and I felt him. I felt the truth of his words.

My father was a Lutheran and raised his family to be active Lutherans too. My siblings and I went to Sunday school, participated in church functions, and attended Vacation Bible School every summer. Team sports, specifically hockey and baseball, were also an important part of my youth, and since my father used to play both sports, he was really involved. After school and on weekends, my father often played catch with me and Mike, or hit balls out to us. "Get behind the ball!" he yelled, or "Watch the ball hit your bat!" He must have been a good teacher because my brother and I were always on our teams' starting line-ups.

One year, he poured us a small ice rink at our acreage, and when we moved to the farm, he flooded our dugout every year to even out the ice surface. He also drove us to the local outdoor rink to play. Pops was a decent player too. He strapped on his old plastic Micron skates and gracefully glided around the ice, scrimmaging with the older boys. These guys played competitively on a regular basis, and my dad had no problem keeping up with them.

My father was a great leader and instilled pride and confidence in me. Even though he had a different way of showing it, he had love for his children—the kind of love that flows through a man's veins and beats in his heart. He wouldn't have hesitated to sacrifice his mind, body, and soul for his children and their needs. He had eternal, everlasting, unconditional devotion to his family. I am still proud to call him my father.

~

My Parents when they just started dating.

My brother only about 6 years old working with my father clearing trees.

My father and sister. Best man and flower girl at Uncle Dougs wedding.

My sister slipping down the slip n slide.

A photo of my parents while they were dating.

Coyote furs on the barn.

One of our last family photos which was taken
about 3 years before my fathers death.

The Family Farm

1- The "bathroom" side of the house where the murder took place
and the tractor was used to pull the body out of the bathtub.

2- The area where the tractor was parked with my fathers
body in the bucket when I arrived home from town.

3- The area in the field where I intercepted my
mothers return from disposing of the body.

4- The location of the dead animal pit where the body was dumped.

5- Some of the fields I spent my day searching in.

My fathers 37th birthday.

The shallow "dead animal pit" that my fathers body was placed in,
and the 2 straw bales that were placed on his body to conceal it.

Here I'm fixing a steel bale feeder. Welding at 14 years old.

My grandfather and I sharing another birthday.

My parents wedding photo.

The Tweety Bird costume my mom made me.

My mom was granted a day pass from jail to celebrate my sisters 14th birthday.
You can see the pain in my mothers face as the rest of us fake smiles.

Michelle at my mothers university graduation. A degree in Criminology – 2005

Celebrating "Day of the Dead" in Mexico. A couple days where
Mexicans believe their loved ones are alive and among them.

Chapter 7

A Week from Hell

I had only been asleep for a couple of hours when my grand-mother came downstairs to the unfinished part of her basement and woke me up.

"What's going on?" I asked, disoriented.

"The police are upstairs asking for you."

What do they want now? I thought.

As I lumbered up the stairs then down the hallway I saw two uniformed cops waiting for me at the door. "Scott, we need to take you in for more questions."

"You've got to be kidding me," I said, glancing up at the clock as I ran my fingers through my hair. It was 2:15 a.m. "Didn't you ask me enough questions last night?"

"I'm sure we did, Scott, but we just have a few things to go over."

Back at the station, I was greeted by the two people I hated most at the time; the male and female officers who had questioned me the night before. Into another interrogation room I went, and another interrogation I got. Instantly, I got bombarded with the same questions. "What time did you get home from Ponoka? What time did you leave for Ponoka? Why did you wait all day to phone the police?"

I gave them the best answers I could. They had all the questions and answers from the night before in front of them on a piece of paper, and any time I didn't answer a question exactly the same way as I had the previous night, they accused me of lying or trying to hide something. I wasn't trying to hide anything. It's absurd to think someone could remember the exact time he drove into his driveway or out into a field for the third time. I told them 10:20 a.m., and they called me a liar because the night before I had told them 10:18. I grew tired and frustrated once again. Those two minutes didn't mean anything to me, but that didn't stop the officers from nailing me to the cross for "changing my story."

Then they hit me with the big questions. "Why did you help your mom carry the body? Why did you help her clean up the house after? How could you dishonour your father's body by putting it in the dead animal pit?" They were still accusing me of helping my mother murder my father, but they had no evidence. Their good cop/bad cop game didn't work. I had nothing to say, and most important, I had nothing to hide.

I could see in their eyes they thought I was guilty. They wanted me in jail.

But they weren't too hard on me this time—they were just annoying. The questioning caused the kind of pain you get trying to sleep with a mosquito in your room. Physical pain—none. Annoyed and not-getting-any-sleep pain—a ton. Receiving no answers, they took me back to my grandparents'. Weak and tired, I again went to bed in the wee hours of the morning.

The next day I woke to the noise of children playing. My little cousins were chasing each other around the basement screaming and laughing. It was around noon, and I had wanted to sleep a lot longer, but with all the noise and commotion I was unable to. My mental clock was all messed up at this point. The sleeping in, staying up late, and eating food at weird times had my body all confused.

I walked upstairs to find the family talking about my mother, who was in the Edmonton Remand Centre; a maximum security prison to which an accused person is sent while awaiting appearance before the court. The police had come earlier that morning and talked to the family about visiting her. It was decided that my brother, my sister, and I would go the next day. The rest of my father's family was still undecided as to whether they wanted to see her. For the first time in a few days, I got to bed early for an uninterrupted sleep.

The next day I woke with a lot of energy. I was ready to take on the day. There's nothing like a good night's sleep and no harassment from the police. The mood in the house was a little less sombre too, though everyone was fairly quiet. I think the whole family was in need of some peace, but at my grandparents' that week there was never any quiet time. People still flooded in with flowers and food. Gift baskets and cards filled the house. I looked forward to seeing my mom, and to getting out of the house.

Just after lunch, we piled into Mike's truck and drove to Edmonton, which was both an exciting and stressful place for us. Everything moved so fast, and there were so many cars. We got lost a few times before we found our destination. That's how farmers are in the city—the big buildings and traffic confuses us.

The Remand Centre was creepy, and I felt out of place. The dull colours, lack of decorations, and sketchy-looking people everywhere made for a sobering environment. We checked in at the front desk and were told to have a seat in the waiting room. Silent and scared, we were facing an experience we knew we would want to forget the minute we walked out.

Twenty-five minutes later, a guard walked into the room and started directing everyone like traffic, sending people into designated rooms. "Mike, Scott, Michelle Hay," he announced as the room echoed with authority. We all stood at the same time. "Follow me." He escorted us to a door and swiped his security card to gain entry. On the other side was a long, narrow hallway filled with what looked like telephone-booth doors. He walked us to the fifth door and told us to wait inside. The little room was barely bigger than a phone booth, so we had to squish together. My brother sat in the only chair with my sister on his knee. I stood behind them, unable to close the door.

My mother was brought in and stood in front of us. She instantly wept at the sight of her children on the other side of bulletproof glass. I could tell she wanted to grab us and hug us. Sitting down, she grabbed the phone and paused before putting it to her ear. She took a second to wipe away her tears and catch her breath. I could see her chest expand and contract as she tried to regain her composure. Mike was waiting with the phone to his ear on our side. Then my mother lifted the phone to her face and spoke to him. As if I had been deaf my whole life, I instantly began reading lips. They talked for a few minutes, then Mike passed Michelle the phone.

"Mommy, when are you coming home?"

My mom's face crumbled. "I don't know, sweetie. Very soon I hope. Just please behave for your grandma and grandpa until I come back. You'll always have Mike and Scott if you need anything." My poor little sister didn't understand the severity of what our mom had done. She just wanted her mommy back. Whimpering and snivelling, Michelle passed me the phone.

"Hi, Scott."

We asked each other how things were going, and we lied to each other by saying things were okay. The conversation was short and the words meaningless. What was important in the moment was just being there. I knew that seeing us would give her the strength to move on. We had barely spoken before the guard yelled out, "Time's up!" We didn't know if we would ever see each other again, or what would come next. We stood, different creatures on different sides of the glass. Knowing we couldn't set her free, my mother sat and cried. Following the guard's orders, my siblings and I turned our backs and walked out. Subdued and quiet, we were escorted out of the Remand Center.

When we got back to my grandparents' house later that day, the police were waiting outside.

"Just ignore them and walk inside," I told my siblings. We had barely started a conversation with the family when the doorbell rang its catchy yet annoying tune.

"Don't worry, it's for me. I'll get it," I told the family. I turned around and walked to the door. My hand reached out to the handle knowing that turning it meant losing my freedom once again. I took a deep breath and swung the door open with force. "Can I help you with something?"

"Yes, Scott, we need to take you in and go over a few things." At this point, this felt like my job. I slowly put on my cowboy boots and jacket. I turned to the family and waved goodbye. I wasn't scared of the police anymore—I was fed up and annoyed.

"Why do you guys keep bothering me?" I asked from the back seat of the police car. "Why do you always pick me up at night? I've told you all I know already, and I'm fed up with this picking-me-up-every-night-for-questioning tactic."

"We're just trying to put all the pieces together, Scott. You act like you don't even care that your father's been murdered."

The evening was uneventful. They held me for a few hours in a questioning room and repeated the same questions. I was actually home by one o'clock.

The next day was tough and tensions ran high as the family started making funeral arrangements. There was a lot of crying and hugging. I was still uncomfortable with all the show of emotion. I wanted to duck out and hide. The priest from my grandparents' church came over. This also made me uncomfortable, as I had never seen him outside of church before. I watched him carefully. *He's probably judging us*, I thought. He gathered us all in the living room. With the exception of my grandmother's soft crying, the room was silent. We all bowed our heads, and the priest said a short prayer. All I could think about was getting out of there. I hated seeing my family in pain. I didn't want to sit there feeling obligated to comfort my grandmother. My emotions had shut down altogether. Drained, I needed out.

That evening, my brother and I got a call from a couple of friends who wanted to go out for beer and a game of pool. We both thought we needed to get out of the house's heavy air and put ourselves in a lighter situation for an evening, so we agreed to meet our friends at a local sports bar. Once there, our moods changed. We started laughing and joking with one another, and we played a few games of pool and had a few drinks. No one talked about the tragedy, and we just acted as if nothing had happened. The night out was exactly what I needed to relieve a little stress. It felt good to get away from all of the crying and questions.

The feeling was too good to be true. Just after midnight, I saw two officers walk in. They walked around the bar slowly, and it appeared they weren't looking for anyone in particular, just doing a routine check. I breathed a sigh of relief and continued my game of pool. Then the officers made their way to the pool tables.

"Are you Scott Hay?"

"Yes."

"We're here to take you to the police station."

I was furious. I couldn't believe they had the audacity to come into the bar and haul me away in front of my friends. How embarrassing. And for what? To ask me more questions? I once again went to work, not because I wanted to, but because I had to.

When I got to the police station the two errand boys placed me in another interrogation room.

After a good hour, I was finally greeted by my mortal enemies, Mr. and Mrs. Asshole, who asked me the same questions over and over again. Finally, fed up, I unleashed. "Do you guys think I don't know what you're doing to me? Every night you haul my ass in here for questioning, thinking and hoping I'll be so tired and drained that I'll confess to murder, or at least to helping my mother commit murder. Your tactics are a fucking joke, and they won't work on me. Somehow you think screaming and yelling at me will work. Well I've been screamed at, yelled at, and beaten down my whole life. I'm immune to this shit. The only thing you two cops are good at is pissing me off and wasting my time. So with that being said, can I go home now?"

The male officer kept his cool, and it looked as if he were pondering his next move in a chess match. The female was not so cool.

"We're just trying to figure out what happened to your father!" she screamed. "You sit there not shedding a tear, talking so ignorantly, and it makes me believe you don't even care about your dad. Going out for drinks with your buddies four days after your dad is killed just shows me you have no heart and that you don't care about the man who raised you your whole life. You make me sick. We're just doing our jobs trying to get to the bottom of this."

"Are you done? Can I go now?" I asked with a smirk, looking her directly in the eye. She glared at me, but it had no effect.

The male officer grabbed her arm and whispered to her, "Let's go," and they walked out of the room.

I sat alone in that room for another hour, wondering what their next move would be. I was proud of myself for standing up to them, and I felt as if they finally understood they could not break me. Finally the two officers who had picked me up from the bar walked in and said, "Okay, let's go."

"Where are we going?"

"We're taking you home."

I had just won a small battle. Mr. and Mrs. Asshole finally gave up.

Chapter 8

Happy Holidays

'Tis the season to be jolly. Two weeks before Christmas, and my family was planning a funeral. Christmas had always been the most wonderful time of the year for me, but instead of enjoying the holiday cheer, I was trying to help my mother find a good lawyer, trying to comfort my family, and trying to help with funeral arrangements. All I was truly doing though was trying to survive.

I went to my old high school to speak to my teacher Mr. Haunholter, an ex-lawyer rumoured to have lost his right to practice law. He was a really cool guy, and one of the very few teachers I felt I could trust. Being back in my school for the first time since I graduated felt a little weird. I didn't want to walk in and see everyone I knew, so I just stayed in the front office and had the secretary page Mr. Haunholter for me. I spoke to him briefly about what had happened, and asked for his guidance in finding my mother a proper lawyer.

"Has your mother hired a lawyer yet?"

"Yeah, she hired Bill Johnson out of Wetaskiwin."

"Well, that probably wasn't a good idea. He has no experience with this type of case. Scott, this is a very serious situation. You need to hire someone who can handle these severe charges." He then wrote down a list of lawyers. Their locations ranged from Vancouver to Toronto. I was pretty impressed by his knowledge of these men, who were considered to be the best in their field. "Hold onto the list in case something happens, but I'm going to make a call to a friend of mine in Edmonton who I feel is the best criminal lawyer in western Canada."

Later that week my siblings and I visited my mother at the Remand Centre again, and she told us about the lawyer who had come to see her.

"I was sitting and talking with a bunch of the other ladies when one of the guards approached me and said, 'Al Nouch is here to see you.' Surprised, I asked, 'Who's that?' and he asked me if Al Nouch wasn't my lawyer. I said no, and he asked me if he should send the man away. But before I could say anything, the other convicts jumped in and told me, 'If that isn't your lawyer now, you should make him your lawyer today. He's the best!'"

Mom ended up being quite impressed with him, and by the end of the week she had relieved her lawyer in Wetaskiwin of his duties. Al Nouch immediately went to work as my mother's legal representative, thanks to Mr. Haunholter.

Now it was time to concentrate on the next order of business; my father's funeral. Up to this point in my life I had only been to two funerals. I had been really young at both of them, so I didn't know how things worked. My family and I called a few friends and told them the date, but it felt as though we hadn't told anyone. I didn't care though— I felt I was beginning to learn to just not give a shit about anything. I had achieved an understanding of the big picture and was realizing that most things in life we get upset over are not worth the time or energy.

The day before the funeral there was a private viewing for just the family. I had no clue what to expect. The whole family drove to the funeral home after dinner that night. My father's casket was sitting open in the middle of the room. Once again, my gut told me not to look. I was scared I might see the cuts on his throat or something gruesome of that nature. I didn't want to see my father dead. I didn't want to see him pale and lifeless, lying in a casket—I didn't want this to be my last memory of him. I wanted to remember him as a strong and powerful figure in my life. I wanted to remember him making jokes and laughing with me. I wanted to remember him alive.

Using the wall as a crutch, I had to remind myself to breathe. I sat back quietly and watched the room, feeling awkward, not knowing what I was supposed to do. A few family members made their way to the casket and stood above him looking down, just staring. *How stupid is this*, I thought. *Am I the only one here who thinks this is weird? We all come here to stare at a dead body like it's some sort of spectacle.* Most of us had never seen a dead body before. Now we were expected to stare at the body of a loved one? It was truly eerie and bizarre.

When my grandmother reached the casket, she let out a loud, haunting cry and collapsed to the floor, hysterical. My uncle and I rushed to her side and helped her up. As she sobbed uncontrollably she grabbed my arm and motioned to me to go see him. I felt forced, but I also knew it was something that had to be done.

I stood tall beside my brother and sister and let them go first. My mouth instantly dried up, my jaw clenched tight, and I ground my teeth. It was as if I were frozen in time. As my brother and sister moved away from the casket, I cautiously walked towards it, then grabbed the side and peered in.

It was now confirmed, in real-life form, that my father was dead. My hands clenched the casket. His body and lips were pale, and his cheeks glowed with a fake rose colour. If only I could have breathed life back into his body. If only he could have said goodbye. I fought back the tears, trying to be strong, but one got away and slid down my cheek. I leaned in close and grabbed his arm, whispering, "I am going to make you proud, Dad. I am going to make you real proud."

The funeral was the next day. It was decided that Mike, Michelle, and I would all arrive in my father's welding rig. We thought it would be a nice tribute to his hobby and career. The rest of the family rode in the funeral home's limousine. When we arrived, I couldn't believe my eyes. The parking lot was jammed with nowhere to park, and speckled with welding trucks. There was a spot saved for us near the front door—we were centre stage for everyone to stare at. As we walked into the church and down the aisle, I kept my head down staring at the floor. I didn't want to see anyone. At the front row, an usher seated me. I don't remember any of the service; I was completely blank the entire time.

As the service came to a close, "Daddy's Hands" by Holly Dunn echoed through the packed church. I bowed my head, fighting back the tears, but the song's chorus rang in my head. *"Daddy's hands, weren't always gentle. But I've come to understand. There was always love in Daddy's hands."* My eyes filled up, and then the dam gave way. I sobbed for a brief moment while telling myself to get it together. *You were raised to be stronger than this. You have to be stronger than this.* By the end of the song, I had wiped my tears from my face, and we marched out to the parking lot and into my father's welding rig. A few deep breaths of the crisp winter air straightened my head out, and I was back on track as we headed to the cemetery. The service there was quick. I had no coat but didn't feel the cold. My father's casket sat above a hole in the ground. The point of no return. *This is it. We're burying him.* I watched as the casket was lowered, back to the womb of Mother Earth, back to the place from which we had all come. A man walked up behind me and draped his coat over my shoulders. I didn't even flinch. As the casket hit the bottom, I heard my auntie cry out, "Goodbye, Bruce."

Daddy's Hands - Holly Dunn

I remember Daddy's hands, folded silently in prayer.
And reaching out to hold me, when I had a nightmare.
You could read quite a story, in the callouses and lines.
Years of work and worry had left their mark behind.
I remember Daddy's hands, how they held my Mama tight,
And patted my back, for something done right.
There are things that I've forgotten, that I loved about the man,
But I'll always remember the love in Daddy's hands.

Daddy's hands were soft and kind when I was cryin'.
Daddy's hands, were hard as steel when I'd done wrong.
Daddy's hands, weren't always gentle
But I've come to understand.
There was always love in Daddy's hands.

I remember Daddy's hands, working 'til they bled.
Sacrificed unselfishly, just to keep us all fed.
If I could do things over, I'd live my life again.
And never take for granted the love in Daddy's hands.

Daddy's hands were soft and kind when I was cryin'.
Daddy's hands, were hard as steel when I'd done wrong.
Daddy's hands, weren't always gentle
But I've come to understand.
There was always love in Daddy's hands.

Daddy's hands were soft and kind when I was cryin'.
Daddy's hands, were hard as steel when I'd done wrong.
Daddy's hands, weren't always gentle
But I've come to understand.

There was always love .....
In Daddy's hands.

The next week my mother was scheduled for a bail hearing. The lawyer thought that they would grant her bail as long as someone could come up with the money. The big question was, who would post it? The day of the hearing, it was decided that if someone posted bail for my mother, she would visit my father's parents immediately after—she had been part of my father's family longer than she had been part of her own. Bail was set at twenty thousand dollars. At first I thought my father's parents would post it, but understandably, it seemed they weren't too interested in helping her out. Instead, my mother's bail was posted by a relative of hers whom I had never met. I wanted to meet this mystery man, curious about who he was and from where he had gotten the money. Why would he help someone he hadn't seen in twenty years? I had so many questions but never got to meet him.

I don't remember who brought my mother to my grandparents' after she was released on bail, but she was there in time for lunch, and was greeted with hugs and questions. The main question was "Why?" I knew this was a question she couldn't answer, and even if she could, the family wouldn't understand. Everyone was crying and no one seemed to know what to do. It quickly became awkward, so my brother and I volunteered to pick up a bucket of KFC for lunch. When we came back we all sat around in the living room eating. *This is bizarre*, I thought. *Here's the lady who murdered their son and brother. She's eating lunch with them, just over a week after she killed him.* I was amazed. The room was silent for the most part, and the tense air suggested my mother had to go. She must have felt it too, because as soon as she was finished eating she got up and hugged everyone goodbye. It must have been a terrible feeling for her, knowing this would be the last time she would ever see this side of her family. It must have felt like saying goodbye to her own parents. I felt sorry for her as she walked out of that house alone—the act symbolized the lonely road ahead of her.

Doug, my dad's best friend and cousin, had offered his family's basement to my mother. I have a lot of respect for Doug. He helped us continuously throughout this hard time. He fed our cows, lent us his farming equipment when we needed it, and never once judged us for what had happened. My mother lived in his basement for the next four months, and that's also where my sister called home. I still feel I could never show Doug and his family enough appreciation for helping my family during that time of need.

I continued staying in my grandparents' basement and tried to be upbeat, but it was tough. People were always visiting, and tears were shed on a daily basis. I would go out with friends as much as possible to keep myself sane.

On Christmas Eve there was still no snow on the ground. This is extremely rare for Alberta. It was a true black Christmas. The symbolism was all too spooky. All of my aunts, uncles, and cousins gathered at my grandparents' house for a gift exchange and dinner. This night had always been exciting, and I was looking forward to seeing my family members smile for the first time in a long time.

I will remember this Christmas for the rest of my life. It affected me deeply and still reminds me of how low things can get. First, the grandchildren opened their stockings, which my grandmother had hung above the fireplace. In mine were some socks and a card with a few lottery tickets. I never won anything, but I was okay with just socks and the card because the real fun would come after dinner, when we would all go downstairs and open the rest of the gifts. Dinner was a feast fit for a king: stuffed turkey, perogies, ham, and potatoes and gravy.

It was a tradition to take family pictures in front of the Christmas tree after dinner. One by one, the immediate families posed. I started to wonder if they would want a picture of my family because it was now just the three of us. As I watched all of my cousins, aunts, and uncles get their pictures taken, I became jealous. I wanted my mom and dad. Missing these two pieces of our family puzzle made me want to crawl into a corner and hide.

"Okay Mike, Scott, and Michelle, it's your turn," I heard my aunt shout out, as if there were nothing wrong. Full of self-pity, I slowly walked up to the tree, then turned around and put on my best fake smile. I looked at my brother and sister and could feel their discomfort too. *I wonder if the room can feel it?* I thought. Cameras started flashing, capturing the first images of my depleted, broken family. I was happy to get out of that room and into the basement, where I thought the mood would change for the better. Don't presents usually make everyone happy?

The family rushed downstairs, the younger kids screaming and running around, wishing out loud for the gifts they wanted. Everyone sat close to his or her family. It felt like the first day of school to me. I didn't know where to sit or whom to sit with, and it seemed everyone was watching me. I couldn't believe I was feeling awkward around my own family. *Just wait for the presents to come and then the entire room will lighten up*, I kept telling myself. My uncle started handing out the gifts. The younger kids opened their toys and games, and their happiness helped the mood. Then the adults began opening clothes, tools, and other trinkets, but I continued to sit empty-handed. My uncle noticed.

"Hey, Mom," he said, "where's Scott's gift?

"It's in a card in the tree," my grandmother replied. My uncle found it and tossed it to me like a Frisbee. It was a gift card for West Edmonton Mall. *This is kind of cool*, I thought. *I can buy what-ever I want.* But I still craved surprise. I wanted to open a gift that was a complete shocker. I had been banking on this surprise to fulfill my need for excitement. I watched patiently as everyone else continued to open gifts. Finally, every person had a stack of presents—trophies. Lying lonely on the floor beside me was my grandparents' card.

Well, this Christmas sucks.

I started sinking into a depression. It wasn't that I was greedy and wanted gifts. It was that this year, a gift would have helped me feel loved, feel as if someone cared. As everyone thanked each other and enjoyed their presents, I stood up and walked to the Christmas tree in hopes of discovering more gifts. Feeling like a coyote searching for scraps, I uncovered a card with my name on it tucked away at the back. I grabbed it and quickly opened it. It was my gift exchange present, from my uncle. A small piece of paper inside read, "Gift Certificate." It was for the local western wear store. I folded it up, put it in my back pocket, and looked around the room. *Doesn't anyone notice I have no gifts?*

My anger built. *My father was just killed a couple of weeks ago and no one can even pretend to care about me.* Feeling invisible, I walked up the stairs with my head hung low, hoping to hear someone call out my name. This didn't happen. I barely made it to the top of the stairs before I began to weep. "Merry Fucking Christmas!" I whispered under my breath as I walked into the dark living room upstairs. The only light came from the Christmas tree. I cried softly, alone in the room, with nothing but the glow of Christmas lights upon my face. The colours were reflected in my tears. I missed my mother. I missed my father. I was angry at the rest of the family. *How can no one be thinking of me right now? How can they just ignore me? How can they treat me like this just after my mother killed my father?* My world was crashing down on me. After a few minutes I regained my composure and wiped my tears away to make sure I showed no signs of crying. I "manned up" and finished the evening by faking every bit of happiness I could show. And that's exactly what it was—just a show.

The next day, my siblings and I packed our gifts and drove out to Doug's house to spend Christmas with my mother. She was in the basement, cooking, when we arrived. We tried to stay upbeat, but I could see my mother falling apart minute by minute. All of us knew this was our last Christmas with her. Cramped in the little basement suite, we tried to have fun and make light of our situation, but nothing in the place was ours. I felt so far from home, even though our farm was only two miles away. We ate a small dinner, exchanged gifts, and took a few pictures. As I look at the photos now, the pain is obvious—fabricated smiles and suffering in our eyes. The drive back to my grandparents' that night seemed to take forever. The sky was filled with stars yet seemed empty.

I had no home. My personal battle was just beginning.

Chapter 9

1998 Unfolds

I rang in the New Year in a horse-riding arena that was converted into a dance hall for the night. All of the farm boys were in attendance, and we got down how real farm boys do—we danced, drank, and got shit on our boots.

Winter had finally hit. With the new year came steady temperatures in the negative twenties and cold spells in the negative thirties. I was getting bored and thought it was time to find a job, so I called up an old neighbour of ours in the pipeline industry. He told me about a job near Rocky Mountain House, starting in the middle of January. This sounded perfect, as I needed to get away from the family and deal with things on my own for a while. Over the next two weeks I packed my bags and prepared for work, and when I got the call, I left immediately. This was going to be an adventure. I had never lived in a work camp before.

I arrived eager to work. *This place is so cool*, I thought. Huge Atco trailers connected to each other to create one enormous hotel with communal bathrooms and showers. The hallways were lined with hundreds of doors, and the rooms were quite small— just large enough for a single bed and a hockey bag full of clothes. Each room also had a tiny ledge and a television connection. I didn't have a television but found it interesting how the camp tried to make the small rooms feel like home for us. This particular camp had no kitchen, so I had to eat all my meals in a restaurant in town. As an eighteen-year-old farm boy who had never gotten to eat in restaurants much, I thought this was pretty cool.

Every morning we piled into a big, blue 4x4 bus for the two-hour drive out to Nordegg County. This was God's country, with beautiful rivers and rolling hills covered in what seemed to be an infinite number of trees. The wildlife was abundant too. I often saw white-tailed deer and herds of elk on the way to work.

On the job, I kept meeting people who had been friends with my father, and they all expressed their condolences and told me what a great guy he had been. That is, everyone except one man—the foreman. When he noticed my name on my hard hat, he asked me the same question all the others had. "Are you Bruce Hay's son?"

"Yup," I answered.

"How's he doing? I haven't spoken to him in a while. I miss the bugger."

Not knowing how to say it nicely, I just came out and told him. "He's dead."

"What do you mean he's dead?"

"He was killed a month and half ago."

The man looked at me, questioning me with his eyes. With scepticism he asked, "How was he killed?"

Once again I didn't know how to put it lightly. "My mom shot him."

"Really?"

"Yup."

In disbelief, the man hung his head and muttered, "Wow. I'm sorry."

I felt bad for him. I could tell he had cared about my father, and this would have been an awful way to learn the news. As he walked away he stared at the ground, his head still low. Then he stopped and turned his head slightly to look at me out of the corner of his eye. I think he was reliving old memories with my dad.

Time marched on as I slaved away, and the shock of my father's death slowly eased. And then I realized that grief is much worse than shock. Living with my grandparents with so many people around, I had been able to bury my feelings about the situation with a faux smile and faux happiness. I had never had time to think about my father's death and let reality sink in. My commute to and from work on the bus gave me the hours needed to dwell on the situation. Most nights before going to bed I would sink into a dark lonely place. Being without a phone and no one to turn to was a test of my strength.

Some mornings on the ride to work, my thoughts got the best of me. I melted the ice on the frosted bus window with my hand, just enough to see the world passing by. As memories of my father filled my head, my eyes swelled with tears. On occasion, the tears got away from me and fell, and I lowered my head, embarrassed, and let it rest on the frozen window. *When will the pain end?* I wondered, hoping no one could see me.

Those mornings, my physical life reflected my mental life— cold and numb. I was thankful for the twelve-to-fourteen-hour days, seven days a week, because at least while I was working, I didn't have time to think about my father.

When the job was finished though, I was happy to head home. Three months alone in the bush with strangers is enough to make any man miss home. I needed to see my friends and family. I stayed at my grandparents' for two more weeks, until my mother, who was still out on bail, rented a place of her own on a shared yard—one hundred and sixty acres of lakefront property. Then I got busy moving our things into storage and getting our farm ready to sell. We had set a date to auction off all the machinery and tools we had acquired over the years. We sold all the cows at Burnt Lake Livestock Auction, and I sold my father's welding equipment privately. All of the money went to an estate lawyer, and from time to time he would give us cheques from the estate. This money kept my immediate family financially stable as we dealt with everything, and to help mask the pain we purchased things we believed would make us happy; old collector cars and new vehicles, motorbikes, snowmobiles, stereos, and lots of clothing. I started drinking more, and the party scene became a regular place for me—temporary pleasures.

I was slowly learning the old cliché. Money would not buy happiness. All the possessions in the world wouldn't fill the empty space in my soul. I was still a sad and lonely boy.

My family should have been in counselling that entire year, but in our farming community, going to a counsellor suggested mental instability. We feared people would talk badly about us, and that we wouldn't be able to hold our heads high. So none of us got any help and we dealt with it alone. Looking back, I realize my family was mentally unstable. Our ignorance was one of the reasons we were in pain for so long. The "be strong and hide your feelings" mentality caused my siblings and me much unnecessary suffering, because we didn't know how to deal with the situation.

My mother's preliminary hearing took place early in the year. It was very private, and the media and public were not allowed in the courtroom for several of the witnesses' testimonies. This didn't stop the media from reporting on it weekly. We might not have been front-page news any more, but there was always a page or column about our situation.

I was one of the witnesses called to the stand, and the experience was weird. I was asked to point out some areas of our farm in photos posted on a huge bulletin board. It was very hard to stay focused because the board not only had pictures of the farm on it, but also more photos of my father's lifeless body. I couldn't look away as I was questioned, and the pictures were always in my view. I often wondered if anyone ever thought about me or the damage they were doing. I don't remember what was said that day, but I will never forget the haunting images.

We got settled into the new place. It was small, and I had to share a bedroom with my mom and my sister. Shortly after, we had a successful auction. People from all over western Canada showed up to bid on our equipment, which was good quality and quite new, and it brought in a pretty penny. Not long after that, the farm sold, and most of the loose ends were tied up. Things were returning to normal—well, as normal as things could ever be. For the most part, my brother, sister, and I had a good summer, considering our circumstances. It was the first summer in six years that we didn't have the farm, which meant it was the first summer in six years that we didn't have a never-ending workload. We felt as though we were on vacation close to home.

Spending time with friends proved to be a good way to keep my mind off my troubles. I rarely faced the fact my father was gone. My brother was by my side for most of the summer, and we drank and laughed our sorrows away the best we could. The people who lived on the same yard site as we did had a child my sister's age, and the two played together every day. My mother got along well with the neighbours, and they often invited us for campfires and sing-alongs. Like all good things though, the summer finally came to an end.

In September, I headed to Rocky Mountain House again— this time to work for a pipeline outfit with which my father had worked for many years. Challand Excavating treated me very well. When I wanted to work, they would put me to work seven days a week for as long as I wanted, and when I told Wade Challand, the owner, that I was thinking about heading home soon, he would tell me it was no problem. "Just go home and spend some time with your mother, and when you want to come back to work, just call me," he'd say. Usually when I called him wanting to come back, he would put me to work within a few weeks of the call. In the pipeline industry this is unheard of, and I'm forever grateful for his sensitivity regarding my situation.

I made some really good friends in the Rocky Mountain House area, the Bosworth family among the best of them. Mr. and Mrs. Bosworth were the most understanding and accepting parents I had ever met, the kind in whom you could confide and trust. Despite their compassion though, I continued to bury my feelings and not talk about my troubles much.

Mr. and Mrs. Bosworth's son and one of their daughters, who were about my age, asked me to go to Mexico with them for two weeks. I had never been anywhere in my life—never been on a plane, never seen the ocean, so the idea of an exotic trip excited me. It would be cheap because we had free accommodation, but I was a little hesitant to accept the invitation because my mother's trial date was quickly approaching. My mother encouraged me though. We were young, naive, and without the comforts of a resort, so when I think back on the trip now, I'm surprised we made it home okay. Some wild things that will more than likely never be spoken of again happened on that trip. One thing I can mention is that I got caught smuggling an iguana into Canada. Thank God they let me go because I had more important business to tend to at home.

Decisions needed to be made regarding the trial: how did my mother want to go about it? Her lawyer had told her he could get her off all charges using personal and family abuse as a defence, but this would cost another sixty thousand dollars, and meant being in court for an additional year. All of the witnesses would also have to be brought back for more questions and cross-examinations. My mother hated bothering people and didn't want to put the family through a long, drawn-out trial, so she decided to plead guilty to manslaughter instead of first-degree murder. Manslaughter carried a minimum sentence of four years in jail. It was now a reality—my mother would be going away for a long time. For the week leading up to the trial we all acted as if nothing were happening; as if my mother weren't going away. We never once talked about the murder, and we never once talked about her going to prison. We were still being true to how we were raised, and in hindsight, I realize how wrong this approach was.

The day came. My mother was about to be sentenced. Her life would be left in the hands of a judge. She walked out of the house for the last time, and we gathered on the front porch for one last family photo; one last picture before the family lost another member. We all tried to smile, but there was no hiding the pain. It's said that a picture is worth a thousand words—well, this one is probably worth more. It tells a story with an ending unknown. Once, there were five flowers in the garden. Now only the three youngest would be left to grow, and their petals were already wilting in the harsh desert conditions. Would they survive the weather to come?

That December, an abundance of snow fell. A new chapter in our lives was starting—a chapter without parents.

Chapter 10

The Details

Throughout the trial and investigation, more and more details about my father's murder were released to the public and to my family. Many of these particulars I didn't want to know, and I still feel my life would be better if I didn't know them. For some reason, my grandmother felt the need to go over these fine points with me. Out of politeness, I would sit and listen to the best of my ability. She always broke down in tears. The details of her son's death will likely haunt her for the rest of her life. I wish the people who had spoken with my family about these details had used better judgment. The following is everything I know about the day my father died and what my mother did.

It was the morning of December 3rd, 1997. My mother and father were planning on going to Wetaskiwin to buy their weekly groceries, do some banking, and visit my grandparents. My father started talking to my mother about paying my grandparents back all of the money he had borrowed from them to buy a tractor. My mother told him that he didn't have enough to do so. The discussion got heated, as my father believed there was money missing from his account. His reasoning was that he had been working a lot, so there should have been sufficient funds. He started pushing my mother around and threw her to the floor while screaming at her and calling her a thief. After things calmed down, my father ran himself a hot bath. And as his mind and body fully relaxed in the tub, he fell asleep.

My mother started cleaning up the kitchen and doing the breakfast dishes. As she worked, her anger and resentment built until it reached a point of no reasoning. She quickly devised a plan to get rid of my father while keeping her family, financial security, and personal safety intact. Her courage grew, and in a furious rage, she walked downstairs and gathered my father's favourite hunting rifle; the Remington 243. Since he had trained her, she knew exactly how to put a shell into it. She loaded the gun and pushed the bolt forward into the firing position, then walked, gun in hand, into the laundry/storage room and grabbed our largest butcher knife. Focused on the task at hand, she let nothing distract her.

She walked up the stairs and into the kitchen unfazed, a mercenary focused on the mission. She placed the knife on the kitchen counter and quietly walked into the hallway. When she got to the bathroom, she peeked through the door and could see my father was sound asleep. She poked the gun through the door jamb and fired one shot into his chest. There was no turning back at this point. She ran into the kitchen and heard my father's bloodcurdling scream. "Susanne, call the police! I've just been shot!"

My father trusted my mother to the bitter end. Many survivors of gunshot wounds say they didn't even realize they had been shot because their bodies went into shock. They claim they didn't hear the bang or even feel the pain. I feel that because my father was an experienced hunter, he knew immediately what had happened. He would have been startled, but he was always cool and calm under pressure. He would have felt the wound with his fingers, and based on the location of the wound, would have known just how severe the damage was.

He would have known this gunshot wound could be fatal, but he was also a fighter, and would have fought until his last breath. He knew that if he was going to live, he had to be rushed to the hospital immediately.

His scream sent chills down my mother's spine, and she knew she had to finish what she had started. She grabbed the knife and ran into the bathroom.

I can only imagine what my father must have felt as he looked up and saw my mother running into the bathroom with the knife. He fought her off briefly as she tried to end his reign of terror, but the internal wounds sucked his life dry until he was unable to fight anymore. The cuts on his hands were evidence of his struggle against my mother before she sliced his jugular open.

As my father's body bled out, my mother pulled the plug and allowed the bathtub to do the same. The walls, the bathtub, and the floor, all covered in blood, told the story. Then she ran frantically to our Quonset, grabbed a roll of industrial poly plastic, and brought it back to the house. She laid it beside the bathtub and began fighting and struggling with the heavy body, but couldn't get it out of the slippery bathtub. She knew that if she couldn't get his body out of the bathtub, she would be unable to dispose of it—she had to think and act quickly.

After briefly analyzing her situation and the surroundings, she ran as fast as she could to our other Quonset, climbed into the tractor, and reversed at full throttle. She drove the tractor around the house and skilfully situated it outside the bathroom window between the trees. She didn't hit the aboveground sewer piping, but she did hit the stucco wall near the bathroom window, leaving a baseball-sized hole. In hysterics, she grabbed the steel chain that was always in the tractor and ran back into the house through the front door. She hooked the chain around my father's body, then opened the bathroom window and removed the screen. Needing more room, she removed the windowpane. As her hands shook in fear, she dropped the pane on the floor, and it punctured the linoleum, creating a small rectangular hole between the toilet and the vanity. She threw the chain out the window and into the tractor bucket before running back to the tractor and hooking the chain to the bucket. She then expertly maneuvered the tractor and its bucket in a way that enabled her to get my father's body halfway out of the tub.

Back inside the house, she unhooked the chain from the body and tossed the chain out the window. She struggled but finally got the entire body out of the tub and onto the poly, which she wrapped around the body. Then with all of her might, she dragged him out of the bathroom and towards the front door. This was a major feat, considering he was double her size. She left the body in the kitchen and ran back outside to the tractor, which she drove to our front step. Thud by thud, she dragged my father's body down three steps and into the tractor bucket. My mother then hid the tractor behind our shop with the bucket high in the sky so that if someone came over, he or she wouldn't be able to see the body in it.

Back in the house, she started cleaning in a frenzy. After finishing the major cleaning tasks, she ran outside to get rid of the body. On her way to the tractor, she glanced south down the road and noticed something that was going to mess up her entire plan.

It was me, coming home earlier than expected.

Not knowing what to do, she thought about making a break for it. Instead, she ran into the garage, backed the car out, and closed the garage door. Before I saw her, she hurried over to the grass to look inconspicuous. She was terribly distraught, but this didn't stop her quick thinking. Immediately, she sent me to the neighbours' to look for my father, and told me to take the ATV because it travelled more slowly than a truck or a car. She then drove the tractor out to our hay pen, where we kept a small pasture and the dead animal pit. After opening the gates to both the hay pen and the small pasture, she dumped the body in the pit. She had to move quickly as there were horses in the pasture, and she couldn't afford to have them get out. With the tractor bucket, she grabbed two large, round straw bales and placed them on my father's body before making a break for the house—and that's when she saw me coming out to the field to meet her. Though the body was gone, she still had some small things to take care of, so she sent me to go see another neighbour and to look for my father in the fields. This would buy her plenty of time to clean up.

She parked the tractor in the Quonset and hurried back to the house. While I was out searching for my father, she burned some clothes in our burn barrel. I assume they were the clothes she was wearing at the time, and any rags used to clean up. The time she spent cleaning was the time she needed to calm down and fine-tune her story, pre-planning answers to the questions she anticipated I would ask. At this point she was like an artist at work. She was focused, and all feelings were gone as she concentrated on finishing her masterpiece.

Finally, I had decided it was time to call the police and family. One by one, people showed up at our house in a display of support. Everyone was told to stay inside as the police searched the surroundings. When the K-9 unit arrived, the police asked for a piece of my father's clothing. I handed them my father's toque so the dogs could sniff out a trail.

One might believe there should have been no trail, as my father's body had been carried in the air for half a mile before being placed among rotting animals. The dogs were amazing trackers though, and from the window in the house we could see them heading out to the field. My mom, likely assuming she was busted, could no longer keep her composure, and she made the first gesture that was out of the ordinary—she started frantically asking the police still in the house if they had found anything. She almost gave herself away. With precision, the dogs directed the police to two areas; the Quonset where the tractor was parked, and the dead animal pit. The police led us to believe they had found nothing, and then brought my mother and me to the Wetaskiwin precinct for questioning.

Over the next few days the police removed the body and examined the house for blood. Microscopic spots were found in the bathroom, on the stairs, and in a clothes chute that led from my parents' room down into the laundry room. All of my father's guns were confiscated, along with the butcher knife.

After my mother confessed, she was charged with first-degree murder. The police continued to suspect she had help, which is why they questioned me for the following week. Approximately eleven months later, my mother pled guilty to manslaughter and was sentenced to four years in prison. The lesser charges were granted because of the years of abuse she'd endured. The judge said he would have given her an even lesser sentence if he could, but four was the minimum.

My sister was sent to live with my father's cousin, Doug. My brother and I lived together at the house on the lake for a short period until I bought an acreage nearby. We visited my mother regularly. She was a model prisoner who completed her high school education and started post-secondary education while behind bars. After serving a little over half of her sentence, she was released on probation.

Afterword:

Scott

Use the darkness of your past to guide you to a brighter future.

I started writing this book out of boredom one summer, with no thought about where it would take me. I was merely putting to paper an experience I could possibly share with my future family some day. The rough draft was horrible, but as I rewrote it and gained some confidence in the story, I started thinking about abuse in rural communities and how people think there is no escape. I thought about speaking to children about how they could possibly stop violence within their own families by talking about their situations. No child deserves to be raised in an environment of abuse, whether it be physical, verbal, or mental. I felt like spreading the word and telling women and children that they aren't trapped—that there is a way out, and that if I had been more vocal when I was younger, I could have possibly stopped a murder. These thoughts helped me push on.

At that point, I had read only one book in my entire life. Yes, you read that correctly. One. Then I started travelling and would spend lazy days and lonely nights reading. I analyzed and absorbed different writing techniques and came home ready to develop my own style. After rewriting the book one more time, I gave it to Larry Harris, one of my high school teachers. He is a published author with whom I had butted heads while in school. I needed to know if the story had potential, and I knew he would be the critic I required. He agreed to read the first chapter and give me his opinion. I sent it to him, and he called me that night to request the entire book. When he was done proofreading it I learned two things: one, it was a grammatical disaster, and two, the story deserved to be told.

★★★

After my father's death, I started drinking and partying regularly to deal with the loss. I ignored and buried the pain, but it would come out in uncontrollable fits of rage or sobbing. Something as simple as a song could trigger a memory of my father and cause an outburst. Sometimes I was embarrassed when my anger took control, and sometimes I just didn't care what people thought. My mind was a mess, and my emotions took me on a roller coaster ride.

Eventually, after countless drunken nights, I realized my life was going nowhere and that I needed to make some changes before it was too late. I sobered up and did some thinking about life and its purpose. I thought about how my father had dedicated his life to hard work and family and decided I wanted to live my life to the fullest…to experience all this world has to offer. My father never saw the ocean. He also never left North America, but he had always dreamed of African animals and loved world history. I thought about how this could be the time to change my life and live in a manner most people only dream about. So I bought a one-way ticket to Uganda.

My soul-searching quest started with four months in Africa, followed by six months in Asia, and five months in South America. It was all the time I needed to settle things with myself. I spent countless hours on buses and planes with nothing but a window and the natural world for entertainment. Staring off into the abyss of life, I asked myself many questions. Should I hate all police officers for what a select few did to me? Should I, or could I, ever trust anyone again after my mother's and father's betrayal? Should I let my mother be a part of my life, or should I punish her by never speaking to her again? Should I resent my father for the abuse I endured? Could I raise my future children to be disciplined without spanking them? What is the purpose of living if we all die anyway? Throughout those months, I gradually came to realize that my father's death was a blessing in disguise, and that my life was better because of it. I became thankful for the realization. I became thankful for the opportunity to truly live a life most only dream of. I became thankful that I could learn from my family's mistakes.

I loved my father deeply, and I still thank him for who I am today. I wish he were here so I could share my countless travel stories with him. I also wish he could see what I have accomplished. But the truth is, I never would have travelled the world if my father were alive. I would have worked hard most of my life and never left North America. I would have settled down young and had a family. I would have been richer financially but not in world experience. I have learned to take massive amounts of time away from work to enjoy life. I travel the world, sleep in, order room service, learn about history, explore jungles, discover cultures, and make new friends.

Today, my mother and I are very close. She has done something most people think is unforgivable, but I feel it is smarter to forgive than hold a grudge. I would rather share my life with one parent, then live a life with no parents. I still have many questions for her, but I won't ask them, because the answers aren't important to me. We are in a good place, and a healthy relationship with her is more important than the answers. As for my brother and sister, the tragedy brought us closer than we could ever have imagined. We are best friends. We have stood by each other through everything, and the bond between us will never be broken. People say it will change as we get older, but we will continue to prove them wrong.

The most important thing I have learned in life so far is that people will always make mistakes. We move on by learning, forgiving, and evolving.

Afterword:

Susanne

. . .for all he had learned, he only hungered more. Every city had taught him something unknown in others. — Peter Brett, *The Warded Man*

> *Mom, I've written a book about what happened with you and Dad. It is my story, from my perspective, of the events that took place, and I would like you to write an afterword for it. I think you would be the best person to do this.*

As I sat absorbing what Scott had just asked me, an overwhelming warmth instantly rushed through my body. For a moment, as I looked at my son sitting across the room, I was at a loss for words, and then tears began to well in my eyes. Scott, you will never know how much this meant to me. I feel privileged and honoured that you want me to be a part of this journey with you. I want you to know with all my heart how very special you are. I am so proud of you for having the courage to write about what happened that horrible, horrible day. I admire you for wanting to share your story with others in hopes of raising awareness about family violence. Children have a right to be cared for, protected, and loved. No family should have to endure the pain ours did. We did not deserve the life we lived, and your father did not deserve to lose his life the way he did.

When you first asked me to write this, I had no idea how difficult it would be to read your story, let alone write an afterword for it. Alone on my back deck one summer morning, I began to read. I didn't make it past the first page before tears were streaming down my face onto the very words that had poured from your heart. I was not prepared to feel the impact of how I had created so much pain in the lives of those I loved so dearly. I devoted the whole day to reading, and I found the intense emotion your words awakened almost unbearable. *I wasn't there for you to comfort you, to hold you and tell you everything was going to be all right*, I thought.

A priest once told me it could take years before I would fully feel the grief in regards to what I had done. "And when that time comes," he said, "your mind and body will know you are strong enough to handle the feelings that will flood through you." I now fully appreciate and understand what he meant. I cannot imagine how confused, alone, and lost you must have felt, Scott. You had no idea what had happened to your father, and yet you were being accused of having a hand in his murder. I cannot begin to tell you how deeply sorry I am to have put you through so much pain. The word "sorry" seems so insignificant. I failed to protect you from the one thing I feared most that day: that you would see what I had done to your father. I will never forgive the police for scarring your sweet innocence. They were wrong. They were so wrong to show you those photos. I understand they had a job to do, but they also had a responsibility to serve and protect the innocent. Scott, you were so innocent, so young, so very alone, and yet you were treated as if you were the guilty one; as if you were the criminal who had callously taken your father's life.

After Scott asked me to write the afterword, it took me a year to put pen to paper. I think subconsciously, I feared the memories and feelings I knew would flood my present self; memories both good and not so good, feelings I thought I had dealt with, and feelings I will need to work through for the rest of my life. Each time I read my son's words I felt the anguish all over again, as if I were reading them for the first time. As I wrote my heart ached, my throat tightened, and I would cry and cry and cry.

I thought about how much pain I had caused my children, and about the abandonment they must have felt and endured. Alone. I cried as I thought about their loneliness, confusion, anger, sadness, and loss. But look at them now. They are so strong. I am so proud. They survived that tragic time in their lives and grew to become the beautiful people they are.

I would like to tell you a little about me. I was born April 11, 1958, in Edmonton, Alberta, the eldest of Dianne and Paul L'Heureux's two children. I don't remember much about my childhood years, but pictures might lead some to believe we had been a happy family. This could not have been further from the truth. On May 28, 1962, my father shot himself in the basement of our home. I had just turned four and my brother, just three. The image of clinging to my mother's leg and seeing blood on her bare feet is forever etched in my mind. We are standing in the middle of the kitchen staring towards the open basement door into the dark. To this day I don't know if this image is real or a fabrication. I never had a good relationship with my mother. We never talked about my father's death. I feel the moment my father chose to leave me is when I began my never-ending search for that perfect, happy family.

It seemed my mother could not stand to be alone after my father's death, and many men, none of whom were worthy of being called Dad, passed through during the course of my childhood. As a result, I have a half-brother and a half-sister with different fathers. My full brother lost his life at nineteen in a head-on vehicle collision. We were very close, and I miss him dearly. He is buried with our father. My mother eventually settled into a common-law relationship with the father of my half-sister, and it lasted over a decade. The man was abusive in many ways. My mother then remarried a man with a drinking problem, but he was very kind, and good to my children. After about eight years of marriage she lost him to suicide as well. He hung himself in their garage.

I was close to both my grandparents but was a Grandpa's girl all the way. I spent a lot of time with him on the farm. I loved being his little helper, and he was always so patient as he taught me the ways of a farmer. This is where my love for the country life originated.

I was embarrassed of my immediate family growing up. I felt we were not a real family; not the family I wanted anyway. We didn't play together, we didn't laugh or have fun together, we didn't talk to each other—we were not happy together. I didn't feel loved, and I couldn't wait to leave. I thought my search was finally over when I started dating Bruce Hay. I spent most of my time with his family on the farm. At age eighteen and five months pregnant, I married him and thought I was well on my way to creating my perfect little family. Instead, my fairy tale became my worst nightmare.

How do you say goodbye to your children? I mean really say goodbye. The day came. I had no idea what my fate would be when I left that sombre November morning to attend my sentencing hearing. I had no idea when I would see my children again. I didn't even know to which prison I was going. This would be the first time my children and I would be apart for an indefinite period of time. I had never felt such pain in my heart. I had never felt such agony flow through my body. The lump in my throat was so large

I felt as if I had to gasp for breath. Helpless, weak, small, empty, I was losing my life. The one thing I feared most above anything else in my entire married life was happening; I was losing my children. How ironic that I was responsible. The image of the three of them standing on the doorstep will plague my nightmares forever. I was leaving them alone, unprotected with no home, a dead father, and a mother going to jail—they were going to be orphans. They didn't deserve the life they had come from, and they didn't deserve the chaos of the years to come. They were innocent casualties engulfed in the senseless war of family violence.

As I climbed into the vehicle to go to the hearing, my eyes never left my children standing there, holding each other up. *Is this really happening?* I thought. As I write this, tears are flowing uncontrollably. My vision is blurring. I am back in time, in that moment. I feel the lump in my throat—I feel my body quivering. Soon I can see only their grey, slumping shadows, slipping from my grasp.

"I'm sorry, my babies, please forgive me! I'm so sorry. I love you! Never forget I love you," I call out. Then I realize nothing is coming out of my mouth. My mouth is so dry. Do they really know how much I love them? What if they don't? My stomach twists, and I feel like throwing up. Never have I felt such heartache. Then they're gone. Gone.

My lawyer and I had agreed to accept a plea bargain presented by the Crown prosecutor. I was charged with manslaughter due to provocation, rather than first-degree murder. The judge said that if I hadn't used a firearm, I would have received a conditional sentence. My lawyer wanted to go to trial using the battered woman's syndrome defense. He was ninety-nine percent sure he would win, but I knew there could be no winners in any circumstance. I couldn't bear the thought of putting Bruce's family and my children through an ugly, drawn-out trial. I had already hurt them all enough. I was sentenced to a minimum of four years in a federal women's institute. I was going to jail.

I learned I would be serving my time at the Edmonton Institute for Women (EIFW). My lawyer knew the warden there and asked her to take me in so I could serve my time close to my kids. My other option was the maximum-security prison in Kingston, Ontario. I felt like a stone statue leaving the courtroom. My body became so heavy I could hardly carry myself. I was devoid of any feelings; I was emotionally spent. My heart was cold, my eyes swollen, my soul empty. I had nothing left to give. I had lost everything. I focused on putting one foot in front of the other, my head hung low. I couldn't bear to look anyone in the face. The guard who escorted me to the holding cells said to me, "It's going to be okay, Susanne. Baby steps. Everything will be okay." Then he gave me a big hug, full of empathy and compassion. It was so totally against all the rules, but so kind. He will never know how much I needed that hug. It felt like a breath of life.

I was shackled, handcuffed, and belly-chained—standard security protocol for a murderer. *How did my life come to this?* I was loaded into the back of a paddy wagon full of other criminals. From this point on, I lost my rights, I lost my identity, I lost my privacy—my life was an open book for all to judge.

I spent two weeks in the Remand Centre before going to EIFW. I was stripped of my personal belongings and put into a heavy, quilted garment called a baby doll after undergoing a body cavity search that left me feeling totally violated. The baby doll was far too large and revealed my breasts every time I dared to move. One of the female guards requested I be issued a T-shirt to wear underneath but was denied because it was against policy where I was going; the psychiatric ward. The police in Wetaskiwin had written "Suicidal" on my file because I was crying all the time. I had just lost everything—my life, my husband, and my children—was this not reason enough to cry? During my twenty years in an abusive marriage, I felt near death many times, but suicide was never an option then, and it would not be an option now. I could not and would never leave my children that way. I was placed in a small room with an inch-thick mat on the floor, a stainless steel toilet, a stainless steel sink, and no blanket.

Two weeks later, shackled, handcuffed, belly-chained, and sporting Remand-issue grey sweats, I was off to the women's federal penitentiary, which I would call home for the next two years. After being stripped and searched again, I was handed grey sweats and a white T-shirt and placed in a unit with ten other women while waiting for a spot to open in one of the eight homes in the prison compound.

Life at EIFW was not what I expected. Yes, a very high chain-link fence with barbed wire coiled at the top surrounded the compound; there were rules and restrictions; the doors locked behind us; we were escorted and patted down by guards from one location to another; there were cameras everywhere; we could only move at certain times of the day; we had to line up numerous times, day and night, to be counted; we were searched all the time; our mail was read and our phone calls heard; we were totally cut off from the outside world; and there was violence, sex, drugs, suicide attempts, "the hole," lifers, and lockdowns. It was a prison. However, we lived in homes, cooked our own food, worked, went to school, attended services at the chapel, had visitors, and shopped from the Sears and Avon catalogues. We had medical attention, psychologists, psychiatrists, therapists, teachers, and doctors; we had a canteen, a gym, a library, and social events, and we could earn certain privileges. This prison was designed for restorative justice. It was designed to support, educate, and help give women the skills needed to successfully integrate back into society as law-abiding citizens.

I was never afraid for my life at the EIFW. As ironic as it may sound, I actually felt a weird sense of freedom. For the first time in my life I felt in control. I made decisions that affected only me, and I had only myself to look after. For the first time in many years, I felt safe. I soon realized many of the women weren't much different from me. We all had stories of pain and suffering. We all had dreams and goals we wanted to achieve. We were all someone's sister, daughter, wife, or mother. We were all women. We were all in jail. I would gain a whole new understanding and compassion for people who find themselves behind bars.

I adapted to the structure of prison life quickly. I did what I was told, as I had always done. My goal was to do whatever it took to get out as fast as I could. I needed to get back to my children. I built good relationships with the women and the staff…I had found myself a family. A couple of girls who had been living on the street adopted me as their mom. Just as there are on the outside, there are roles and ranks established in jail. These girls were part of a tough group—well-known, seasoned inmates respected by some, disliked by some, and feared by some. They said they would take care of me, but I really didn't need their protection. I was one of the older inmates at EIFW and had come from a pro-social background, unlike the majority of the women. I had no substance abuse addictions, I did not smoke, I did not gossip, I was friendly with everyone, I was a good listener, and I minded my own business. I had nothing to hide and no one to be afraid of but myself.

Four correctional officers were assigned to my case, and they helped develop a reintegration plan to address the underlying factors that had led me to kill my husband. First, I needed to understand why I had stayed in an abusive relationship for over twenty years. Second, I needed to learn how to care for myself and communicate my feelings. And third, I needed to focus on education. I treated my time in prison as a serious opportunity to become strong and healthy so I could be there for my children when I got out. I knew that never again would I have this isolation to dedicate all the time I needed to myself without any of life's everyday stresses. I enrolled in all the programming I could, attended various forms of therapy weekly, and completed my high school diploma within my first year inside.

I worked in the prison's library, chapel, stores, commercial arts program, and maintenance department. I planted and cared for a garden and flowerbeds. I became a member of the Peer Support Team, and inmates called upon us 24/7 to help them work through issues. This was my most valued role. Many of the inmates trusted me and cared about what I had to say. I eventually became chair of the Peer Support Team, as well as chair of the Inmate Committee. Staff called on me when women tried to commit suicide, and when they were put into "the hole." The hole is the segregation unit, where women are isolated from the general population. There are two types of segregation: disciplinary and administrative detention (to protect prisoners from the general population). The cells in this unit are very bare, and prisoners are usually fed through slots in the doors. They have minimal contact and access to everyone and everything.

Ultimately, my loyalty was to my fellow inmates. I was really good at keeping secrets—I had been keeping them my whole life. I grew to care about the women, to understand them. They needed to be heard and to know that someone cared enough to act on their behalf. All they needed was to be loved, and I knew how they felt. After all, my whole life, I had sought to be respected and loved for who I was, not who someone else wanted me to be.

In prison, I was allowed to be myself. I vowed I would never tell another lie. I had lied my whole life to avoid my husbands' anger, and my children had learned to lie to avoid their father's anger. Sadly, I had supported those lies. Now, I wanted to be free. I wanted to be true to myself and my children.

After serving ten months of my sentence, I applied for early parole. Everyone thought I would get it—I had taken part in all the necessary programming and therapy, and I had been the perfect inmate. I was so sure I was getting out.

The parole hearing was like being on trial all over again, and to make matters even more uncomfortable and intense, the Hay family was seated right behind me during the whole process. I was denied. "You're still too disconnected from your crime and the impact it had on others," the parole board told me. I was devastated. The prison had granted me special permission to see Michelle after visiting hours so we could celebrate. There would be no celebration. We cried and cried in each other's arms—what seemed like hours was only minutes. She was unable to understand why we could not be together, and I had no answers for her. My little girl needed me and I had failed her once again. It would be another eight months before I could apply for parole again and at that moment, it seemed like an eternity.

The kids visited me as often as they could, along with other family members and friends. The prison staff told me I had more visitors and received more mail than any prisoner they had known. I was very fortunate. But the goodbyes were the harsh reminder of where I was. Michelle and I talked on the phone often. Sometimes we would work on her homework and sometimes she would just cry about how much she hated where she was staying. My heart ached for my little girl. Eventually Michelle was able to stay with me for a Private Family Visit. This was another privilege that could be earned. In the compound was a small yard with a cabin in which we could spend three days and evenings together. This time was very special to me, and I tried to reassure my daughter that everything would be all right and that when I got out, we would start a new life with each other and it would be such an adventure. In my final year I was also granted Unescorted Temporary Absences, during which I could leave the prison and stay with someone who had been preapproved to host me as long as I reported to a parole officer daily at a particular time. On one of these visits my children and I celebrated Michelle's fourteenth birthday and on another we celebrated Mike's twenty-fourth birthday. We would never talk about what had happened and just enjoyed the little time we had together. I missed my children so much.

After being denied early parole, I decided to focus all my attention on school and therapy. I had to get back to my children. I dropped all my committee involvements except for Peer Support Team, and was granted permission to see a therapist out in the community so I could build a relationship with him before being released. I had learnt that therapy was a good thing, not something to be ashamed of as I had always thought. I needed someone to help me make sense of my thoughts and behaviours.

In prison, I learnt so many different ways to channel my negative energy, my hurt, my sadness. I had to get to know myself all over again, and learn to love who I was. I learnt different ways to care for my mind, body, and soul. I learnt how to analyze and understand why I felt, thought, and reacted to situations in certain ways. I took part in music therapy, dance therapy, art therapy, and creative writing. I learnt ancient forms of therapy such as how to read Tarot cards and runes, which have more to do with how you interpret and understand your own thought process, than fortune telling. I learnt about Native spirituality and participated in sweat lodge ceremonies and round dances. I learnt how to do tai chi and yoga, which also help channel negative energy into healing and a positive experience. I learnt to listen to my body and be aware of how I felt. The more I learnt about all the forms of healing and caring for yourself, the further I felt myself move away from the traditional religions I had been raised with. I began to realize the philosophy of sin, guilt, damnation, and punishment was not what I wanted. It was not conducive to loving myself, it did not help me nurture myself, and it did not allow me to forgive myself. I wanted to be the best person I could be—I owed this to myself, I owed this to my children, and I owed this to the memory of Bruce's life.

I enrolled in a couple of university correspondence courses. No, the government does not pay for a prisoner's university degree, but it is responsible for an inmate's high school education. I wanted to be prepared to go back to school as soon as I was released. Since I was a child I had wanted to be a social worker and help make others' lives better. I took Sociology 101 and Psychology 101, along with an English upgrade course. I was also granted permission to participate in a work release program. Through these programs, prisoners are allowed to go out into the community and gain employment experience. I was not paid, and I had to return to the prison before four p.m., in time for face count. First I was a receptionist in a massage therapist's office, and then I took a position in a legal studies program at the university.

Bruce had always told me I was stupid, and that I would never make it "out there" on my own or amount to anything without him. "You are a waste of skin and a waste of the air you breathe," he would say. I had very low self-esteem and lacked self-confidence tremendously when I first went to jail, but the more I accomplished, the more I believed I could do anything I put my mind to. I had something to prove: I had to prove I could think for myself, that I was intelligent, and that I could contribute to society in a meaningful way. And I did. I started speaking with the prison pastor out in the community. I shared my story and tried to relay the tragic dynamics of family violence. I participated in various activities during Restorative Justice Week that year and was invited back to the prison for many years after to share my experience of being in jail and discuss how I was coping in the outside world. And after my release, I developed a volunteer program to benefit women in the maximum-security unit.

When my next parole hearing came around I was prepared but just as intimidated as I had been before the last one. However, this time I was much more confident and was able to show the parole board I had achieved a deeper understanding of what had prompted me to commit such a violent crime. More important, I had a deeper understanding of how my actions had affected many people—people I love. The ruling was in my favour, and I was granted day parole under the supervision of my mentor (a nun). I was to spend the next six months in her home, which happened to be a convent, and my daughter was welcome to spend this time with me. I was ecstatic! I was released on November 22, 2000.

And then the completely unexpected happened: I found myself in a relationship with a woman. This was not a relationship that started in prison, contrary to popular belief. Jane had been on the Peer Support Team, and I confided in her often during my early days in prison. She listened, was intelligent, and always offered good advice. We became friends, and then four months later she was released. I didn't realize my feelings for her were stronger than friendship until long after she was out in the community. We corresponded and got to know each other over the next year and a half I was inside. She made me feel special; she made me feel as if she would do anything for me; she made me feel as if I were the only person in the room, as if I were the only woman in the world. I felt so alive, so young, so fresh. She gave me everything that Bruce hadn't. She gave me everything I needed at this time in my life. She let me be myself.

I learnt to hate labels during my time in prison. Inside, people are categorized by number and last name: Hay, inmate #126202E. Everyone tries to put you in a box that doesn't quite fit. The boxes make organizing easier. They allow for risk management, control, and power. And they simplify all processes that lead to the inmate's release. As long as you conform to a box, they will know what to do with you. I was lucky, I had a good team—but I never agreed with the whole labeling process. No psych test ever had the answer that would allow me to accurately describe how I was feeling, so I was always concerned I would be misdiagnosed. So in terms of labels, am I a lesbian? No. I feel quite privileged, though, to have experienced long-term relationships with both a man and a woman. The experiences made me a more well-rounded individual with an open mind for those who are different. They made me even less judgmental and more accepting. They made me realize love has no boundaries.

As soon as Michelle and I got settled into Sister Mary's home, I knew I needed to tell my daughter about my relationship. I was not going to start my new life on a lie. In the first week I was released, I took Michelle to Jane's apartment, and we broke the news. I immediately wished I could take back what I had just blurted out as I watched all the life drain from Michelle's face. Her blank stare bore holes right through me, and her little body seemed to curl up into the fetal position in her chair. I sensed she just wanted to disappear. Michelle and I had waited two long years to be together, and I had promised her that it would just be the two of us starting a new life together. What had I just done to my little girl? Here I was responsible again for crushing her heart.

Before I could tell her brothers myself, she phoned them immediately when we got back home. I don't remember hearing from Mike but I do remember vividly the call from Scott that broke my heart. Sitting on the kitchen floor with the phone to my ear, I listened to my son rip me apart.

"I was so excited and proud. I wanted you to meet my friends in Calgary. How can you do this? Your priority is taking care of Michelle. She needs you. Being alone for the rest of your life is your punishment for killing Dad. Your children should be enough to make you happy." Then he told me I would have to choose between my relationship with Jane and them. I hadn't seen Scott yet, and I ached to hold him. I missed him so much in that moment.

But I would not see Scott again for ten years. Ten long years. I saw Mike twice during that time, and I kicked Michelle out of the house a year and half after I was released, for acting out. I didn't blame her though. I just wasn't strong enough to deal with her behaviour. I spent my first Christmas out of prison alone. I couldn't even be with Jane because I was on day parole and she was in

Calgary, which was outside my travel jurisdiction. Once again I had lost my children, but this time, it seemed more like my own choice.

I would grow to deeply regret my decision in many ways. The timing was so wrong. My focus should have been on healing myself and my family. We needed that time to get to know each other again and learn how to be a family. I will never be able to convey to my children just how sorry I am for my choice. I should have been there for them. We should have been together. Throughout those years though, I never lost hope that we would be a family again someday, and this hope drove me to continue pursuing my goals and dreams.

I decided that all I could do was continue on my journey, hope to lead by example, and parent from a distant place—my broken heart. Professionals and friends said I needed to stand up for myself, that I couldn't allow the children to dictate how I lived my life, that I had to be strong and learn to live my own life before I could learn to be a good parent. But the advice didn't stop me from constantly wondering if I had made the wrong decision. And it did nothing to ease the pain and emptiness in my heart.

In January 2001 I enrolled in courses at the college with the hope of being accepted into the university's Bachelor of Arts program in a year and half. In February I got a part-time job at a greenhouse, making seven dollars an hour. The job was relaxing and rewarding. I felt needed and valued, and gardening had always been a comfort for me. That fall, a professor whom I had met while in prison, called me. We had both sat on the EIFW Steering Committee—I as the inmate representative and she as chair of the committee representing the community. The department at the university had just received the funding to make my previous position permanent. *Is this really happening?* I thought. I felt accomplished, I felt successful, I felt important: I would be working at the university. I was proud of myself.

The professor was a lawyer who strongly believed in social justice, and she walked the talk. I have the utmost respect for her, what she stood for, and what she worked so hard to accomplish: justice for everyone. I owe a tremendous amount of gratitude to her for the person I am today and for where I am in my life. She is my unsung hero.

I was eventually accepted into the Criminology program, and I will never forget my first day on campus as a student, in the fall of 2003. It was a beautiful day with a slight breeze, and rays of sunlight filtered through the one-hundred-year-old trees. I, Susanne Hay, was fulfilling one of my dreams—I was going to university. I was going to be okay.

I graduated May 2005. It was a milestone for me, and an accomplishment I was fortunate enough to share with my daughter. As I accepted my degree on stage, I heard a loud and clear, childlike voice shouting, "Yahoo, Mom! That's my mom." As one of the dignitaries shook my hand, she said to me, "Someone is very proud of you."

"Yes, that's my daughter," I said with tremendous pride. My relationship with Michelle had been difficult throughout those years, but we always managed to hang on to each other. I can't help but admire her maturity, courageousness, and strength. She was always there for me no matter what. Except for that first year, she spent Christmas with me no matter how uncomfortable it was for her. She always remembered my birthday and even organized my fiftieth birthday celebration all by herself.

Today, we have a very special relationship; an unbreakable bond. Through the turbulent years, it only became stronger and more meaningful, and it has matured to an unmatched level of security, strength, and comfort. We have grown together to become best friends, and I could not be prouder of the young woman she has become. I could never thank her enough for her constant, unconditional love.

I realize now that those ten years apart from the boys benefit-ted us all in so many ways. Though I feel we should have been together, I also know we needed to grow individually. Our lives on the farm weren't really our own. It seemed none of us had much choice about what we did—we worked hard and had little free time. We felt guilty and ashamed whenever we had fun, and we even laughed when we felt like crying. We all felt responsible for trying to keep the peace to avoid Bruce's temper. We also felt responsible for trying to please him. We lived our lives for Bruce, trying to find our happiness through his happiness. We allowed ourselves to feel controlled by his anger. We desperately sought his love and approval, not realizing we would never achieve it because we did not love ourselves. We had no communication skills, we said things we didn't mean, and we didn't know what we meant. We lied to protect and cover up for each other, and we lied to protect ourselves. We didn't trust ourselves, we didn't trust our feelings, we didn't trust our decisions, and we didn't trust other people. We lived co-dependent lives and lost touch with our own needs and desires.

In our ten years apart, we had the freedom to make bad deci-sions and good decisions, and had no one to blame but ourselves. We became wiser and healthier. During that time, hope continued to thrive in my heart—hope that we would come together again as a family, stronger and full of love. Hope motivated me, kept me strong, gave me courage, and pushed me to reach out.

The year 2009 would prove to be our turning point. If there was anything I was sure of, it was my love for my children, and I needed them to know. With Michelle's encouragement, I decided to wish my boys a happy New Year. I called Mike first, and he then passed the phone to Scott, as they happened to be at the same party. Before writing this afterword, I looked back in my journal and could feel the fear and excitement in my words:

Jan 1, 2009

A Happy New Year! I spoke to my boys today. I wished them a happy New Year and I told them both I loved them and I missed them. I then asked them to be a part of my life and they both agreed it was time. I am so hopeful right now—I am so happy they both talked and talked about themselves without me asking. It was amazing. It was my Christmas miracle and I couldn't have asked for anything more. I will never forget what Scott said to me: "If I ever had children I would want you in my life." Tears rolled down my cheeks. These were precious words to my ears. My sunshine was just beaming inside. Both boys made me feel so special today. I couldn't believe what was happening. We are on the right path. Our lives will change this year.

On February 25, 2009, I called Mike again, and he sounded genuinely happy to hear from me. Another sigh of relief. That week we met in Sherwood Park for lunch. As soon as I drove into the parking lot I could sense Mike's presence. I was so afraid I would not recognize my son, and yet, my heart knew he was there. As I walked into the Country Garden restaurant at the Flying J, I heard a *psst* behind me. I turned around and there was Mike, as I had always remembered him. I looked into his eyes and felt his smile. Tears welled up in my eyes, and we hugged. I could feel our love. We had a great lunch. This was the beginning of a new and wonderful relationship with my eldest son. I am very proud of the man Mike has become. He is strong, dependable, confident, honest, kind, and very intelligent. He is accomplished in his career, owns a nice home, and has a beautiful little family. I had the honour of being by my son's side during the delivery of his first child. It was a special and unforgettable moment. My first-born holding his first-born—there are no words to express my absolute love for him that day. What an exceptional act of forgiveness my son displayed in allowing me to share this moment with him. My first grandchild enjoys a lot of love. I am happy to have my son back.

My first meeting with Scott would not come until later that year. I had anticipated he would be my biggest challenge. Although we did talk over the phone a few times, I could always sense his apprehension, though I could also feel his willingness to try. I was okay with that. I had waited too long to have him back in my life to rush things now. After all, I had crushed his trust in me. I would have to gain it back slowly. I had a lot to prove to my son, and my actions would mean more to him than anything. I needed to show him I was ready to be the mother my children needed me to be. I needed to show him I had the strength and commitment it would take to make our family whole once again.

The day finally came. Scott would be coming for dinner. The last time I had seen my son was on an unescorted prison pass—exactly ten years ago. I was so scared yet bubbling with excitement. As I write this and try to think of the words to explain how I felt, tears roll down my cheeks and onto my lap. That day is engraved so deeply in my memory; the past becomes the present.

I hear his motorbike roll around the corner and come to a stop in the driveway. My breathing quickens and my heart beats out of my chest. I am smiling from ear to ear as I run to the door to greet him. Nothing could have prepared me for what I see. As my eyes rest upon his face for the first time, a flood of emotions rushes through my body: *Oh my God, he looks so much like his father!* Surprisingly I welcome the resemblance with a sense of long-lost love.

"Oh Scott, Scott." I draw him into my arms and we hold each other. As I tremble, I feel the strength in his arms and the intensity of our longing for each other for so long. I have missed him so much. We finally let go, and he introduces me to his girlfriend. I apologize for being so emotional, but at the moment I have no control. I am just so overjoyed to see him. I feel like the luckiest mother in the world. All of my children have come home.

My relationship with Scott has grown into something I had only dreamed it could be. As we spend more time together getting to know each other as adults, I discover we have so much in common. We find comfort and contentment in each other's company. We have a relationship that doesn't always require conversation; one that allows us to just be in the moment and enjoy where we are. We understand each other and accept each other without judgment. We work well together and have had fun doing the work, unlike when we worked on the farm together. We have helped each other landscape our yards, I have helped him paint, pack, and move, and Scott does many chores around my home that I cannot do. We both enjoy the wonders of nature and what the raw land has to offer. We both relish and appreciate the beauty of the little things in life. I guess you could say we both believe in taking time to "smell the roses." We both believe in natural and spiritual alternatives to achieve a better quality of life. We both love to explore new lands, and believe in submerging ourselves in other cultures.

Scott has travelled the world extensively, and I can see the maturity and wisdom this has brought to his character. We spent a month in Africa together living with the locals. There are no words to explain the beautiful bonding experience we shared and the pride I feel with the growth of our relationship. He also took me to Mexico, where he taught me how to snorkel. I am so proud of how open-minded and nonjudgmental he has become. He has compassion for humanity and a passion to bring community back into his life. He has the same desire for family as I have always had. He has a positive outlook on life and never backs down from a challenge. He is adventurous, welcomes new challenges, and commits to facing his fears. He strives for a better life and seeks to enjoy life in the moment. I think it is so sweet that Scott includes me in his future plans, and I am touched by how he feels responsible for caring for me as I grow older. I am very appreciative of how our relationship has grown, and of how close we are today. I am thankful for his love, and so very grateful for his forgiveness.

I know you likely have more questions as you read this. How could I kill the father of my children? How could a loving relationship deteriorate into something so devastatingly tragic? I read a pamphlet once called, "Breaking the Pattern", it was written by women in their voices, telling their stories— so much like my own. There was some comfort in knowing I was not alone but also sadness in knowing there were so many. There are no easy answers. However, we do need to achieve deeper levels of understanding into the warlike dynamics of family violence and the behavior associated with it. Bruce and I had a mutual dependence that kept us together and filled some strange need for both of us. Eventually though, it became harder and harder for me to anticipate what he wanted. I began to feel inadequate, as though I had failed as a wife and mother. I couldn't please my husband, and I couldn't protect my children. I thought I needed to try harder to be a "good wife." The harder I tried, the less I felt he respected me. The more he blamed me, the more I blamed myself. My feelings of guilt, shame, and helplessness consumed me. I felt powerless and inadequate. I tried harder to anticipate his moods and reactions. This was the only control I had.

I didn't leave because I feared he would carry his threats out. There wasn't a "rock small enough to hide under." He "would find me and kill me," and he knew "people who could do the job." Of course the ultimate threat was that he would take the kids away and I would never see them again. I believed him.

Most people don't understand how powerful the cycle of violence is, or how strong our bond was. People on the outside might find it hard to understand that our need for each other was as powerful as our need to break away from each other. We felt trapped within the volatile love and devastation of our relationship.

I know there are many of you who will read these words and know exactly what I mean when I compare my life to a war zone. I lived day by day, sometimes hour by hour, always in the moment, dodging some bullets while always knowing I couldn't keep it up for long. I never knew when the next bomb would fall. I questioned every decision as though my life depended on it. It was never the right one. Everything that went wrong escalated into crisis proportions. I spent sleepless nights in the darkness wishing the quiet would last forever, and often that the morning would never come.

There is no excuse for family violence. Innocent children don't deserve to feel adult pain. The person I am today would have had the strength and the courage to leave, and the confidence to know we would survive on our own and be okay. There is no doubt in my mind: if I could go back in time and change what transpired that day, I would. There is not a day that goes by that I don't wish my children had their father in their lives again. I am truly sorry for the pain I caused everyone.

That being said, I have come to believe events in our lives happen for a reason. We may not always understand why in the moment, but eventually we do. What's important is that we learn from the past. How we choose to move forward with our lives determines our destiny. I believe Bruce is proud of our accomplishments. I believe he is proud of how strong his family has grown to become, and of the fact that we are together once again. I also feel he appreciates how we strive to fulfill his goal in life: for his family to be the best it could ever be.

My home is now a home the kids and I have built together— a home in which they have all spent time, and a home shared only with them. It's a home in which we have Christmas, a home in which we play games, a home in which we eat, laugh, and cry. It will be a home my grandchildren will know as "Grandma's house"; a home filled with warmth and happiness. It was always my dream to build a feeling of home again. By no means do I want to forget or replace our old home, but we need to create a new one with love and acceptance.

Each child has a special place in my heart—different but the same—and that is where home is and will always be, no matter where we are. I am so proud of my children for persevering through the tragedy that fell upon our family that dark December day, and I know their father is very proud of them as well. We have grown into a beautiful family; a loving family; a happy family. This is the family I have been searching for all my life.

I feel this book will encourage us to talk—talk about things we haven't wanted to mention, about things we don't understand, about things that may hurt, about things that make us happy. Just talk. I feel this book will bring us even closer together, as a family. For this, Scott, I thank you with all my heart.

Resources

The National Domestic Violence **Hotline** | 24/7 Confidential Support
www.thehotline.org

Kid's Help Phone1–800–668–6868

Women's Web –Violence against women and children: resources
http://www.womensweb.ca/violence/resources.php

National Domestic Violence Hotline1–800–799–7233
NDVH (TDD)Telecommunications Device
for the Deaf1–800–799–3224

Canada: domestic violence information « HotPeachPages International
www.hotpeachpages.net/canada/index.html

Assaulted Women's Helpline
www.awhl.org

For more information about *Bleeding Hearts* and its author please visit www.bleedingheartsbook.com

Bleeding Hearts
www.bleedingheartsbook.com

Cover painting by Nadine Shenher, Canadian Abstract Artist
www.nadineshenher.com

Nadine Shenher's abstract contemporary paintings carry a pure
energy and demonstrate her commitment to the creative process.
Her artistic philosophy is based on high vibrancy, which defi-
nitely is accomplished with her bright and bold art. Her greatest
joy is taking the beholder on a unique, interpretive experience.